TRAGEDY AND INNOCENCE

*consisting of a treatise on the psychology of
tragedy together with an essay on the vision of
William Blake, the two comprising a study in the
nature of myth, symbolism and consciousness*

Harvey Birenbaum

to

the memory of

Ned Adelsohn

and those of us who

were alone together

CONTENTS

v

WHAT FOLLOWS

I like to think of what follows as a sketch of my orientation in reality. I take reality to be the reality of experience, our subjective existence, not for any metaphysical reasons but because experience in this sense is the way in which we have ourselves that really matters most to each of us day by day. It is the realm in which our main problems and opportunities lie. It is what we have to work with most immediately, mediating all of our activities. It is the way in which we have art.

It is particularly important to me that literature can be understood only in terms of its relation to life--not so much as the reflection of institutions or events or types of people, but as part of the process of felt and aware life as it occurs generally and as it evolves especially during our experience of ourselves reading. An essential feature of typically human life is the imaginative or (more broadly) symbolic process. Literature exists in a symbolic continuum between the mind imagining it and the work imagined in itself, a continuum of projection which determines its nature. The meaning of a work depends, therefore, upon its existence as a work; the play depends on the kind of reality that language can create. But it also depends on its relation to our consciousness, a particular relation that it is endowed with by virtue of its stylization; and that relation is determined first off by the nature of consciousness itself. Every symbol is controlled by its particular symbolic kind of relation to the rest of reality. From this point of view, what follows can be considered an exercise in the study of experience, of consciousness, of culture, and of the nature of relationship.

The two parts of this book focus, from two directions, on interdependent extremes of experience and of literature. There is first a treatise on the psychology of tragedy, and there is secondly an essay on Blake and symbolism in which each side of this double topic, Blake and symbolism, provides an opportunity for writing about the other. By putting these two essays together, I have tried to lay out various formulations that make up a basic complex, including several concepts of myth with some of their implications. My most ambitious reason for doing so was to try to impress upon myself what I take to be true. Of course, I have also wanted to provide some other people with this framework within which they might contemplate their own assumptions.

The material on tragedy and the material on Blake should complement each other in several ways. Basically, human experience is seen first from the tragic perspective and then from the ecstatic, so that some insight into consciousness itself may emerge from their interrelation. But also, a broader theoretical approach in the first part is followed by a particularized practical study in the second, sustained through a different kind of theoretical discussion. There is also first a focus on myth as a condition and then a focus on myth as an activity--or to put it otherwise, a focus on vision in relation to "content" and on vision in relation to technique.

The works of Blake provide an especially clear, but not a special, case in the relation of literature to life. It is an act of self-satire to study his work merely as a critic or scholar, without a serious concern for the nature of vision itself, which breaks down distinctions between content and technique, art and life, altogether. What Blake sees as visionary, and others more or less have seen before him and since, is a shape of reality that informs all of the issues I am groping towards.

Reviewing such basic material so briefly, the method should work suggestively. I hope I achieve more by implication than by assertion. I like leaving the material on tragedy without a great deal of specific application so that a reader can test it directly against his or her own experience and perhaps recreate aspects of its significance directly.

The reader will sense, I hope, that some movements of the discussion are meant to be more assertive than others and some more experimental. On the level of implication toward which the material ultimately moves, I find myself taking it most seriously and least seriously at the same time. It is the level at which

ix

notions from different directions impinge on one another to suggest what is not spoken, a coherence prior to language, theories and systems. It seems to me that this understanding must be a matter of clear and simple truth, a knowledge though nothing new, more firm than dogma, and yet a sort of speculation that is particularly useful if it is taken only tentatively. But perhaps this dilemma hints at the method of myth itself.

To deal with the arts and other forms of expression that communicate qualitatively (and with the even less explicit truths of immediate experience) we learn to check ourselves by a tentative method of assertion. We remember that certain kinds of truth only tend to be true and are betrayed by absolute affirmation. They require what Philip Wheelwright calls (in The Burning Fountain) "soft focus" and "assertorial lightness." We can make the scholar's choices that the poet never had to make and proliferate objective discriminations. Sometimes, however, it can be most accurate to generalize, to clarify what must be true. This is to evoke--or to invoke--myth by picking up the form of an organic rhythm, a form that can be obscured so easily by the factual goal-seeking mind lighting little rooms of space. A myth of the future can be a sensitive account of the present; the supernatural is a potently expressive projection of the wholly natural. Blake himself insists upon a defense of the specific and concrete:

> To Generalize is to be an Idiot To Particularize is the
> Alone Distinction of Merit--General Knowledges are

those Knowledges that Idiots possess
(Annotations to Reynolds)

But surely it is easier to see in his work a contrary truth which is yet not the abstraction that he is so stoutly opposing.

What _must_ be true _is_ true in a special sense, no matter how much evidence can be adduced against it. What I mean is not a matter of the wishful thinking we usually call our beliefs but the structure of reality that underlies all the ambiguities, contradictions and obscurities of fragmented data and that sheds significance upon other kinds of truth. It is one of the functions of literature and of myth understood _as_ myth to convince us of what must be so by having us participate in its forms. Myth and art (and my discourse too, hopefully) can induce assent although they do not try to prove anything. We sense the structure of our experience in such a way that we are aware of its appropriateness. The phenomenon through which this consciousness comes to us blends what is personal with what is both within and beyond ourselves, confirming the self-sufficiency of our insight, its general truth. This phenomenon is the experience of symbolic projection and symbolic communication; in both of these terms it leads us at the same time into ourselves and into a realm to which we only belong.

Some of the few notes to the text indicate parallel discussions that I found after most of my work was done, but

xi

others--at least those to Zimmer, Campbell, Langer and Laing-- understate the influences on my work and its (inevitably, fortunately) derivative nature--the dedication much more so. While I was working on the Blake piece, Allen Ginsberg's tunes to The Songs often played in my mind, leading the way. I am very deeply and personally grateful to many of my graduate students at San Jose State for their serious response to this material during its development, especially those who lived through what one participant called a seminar in applied tragedy. The original manuscript was completed during a year's visit to the University of East Anglia, at Norwich, where I benefitted from the discussions and suggestions of my friendly colleagues. Back home at San Jose, I have been very fortunate in the support of my department, during times when better books cannot easily get published. Dennis Chaldecott, Rex Burbank and Nils Peterson were especially helpful when my tardiness in publishing caused professional difficulties. Paul Privateer gave the manuscript a useful final reading. Leslie and Paul Calandrino performed nobly on the word processor to prepare the final text. From another part of the country, Robert W. Corrigan gave me a very welcome boost when he included a portion of this book in the second edition of his anthology Tragedy: Vision and Form. I am grateful to the Trustees of the British Museum for their permission to reproduce Blake illustrations from their collection.

1973, 1982

THE CELEBRATION OF DISASTER

Notes on Tragedy

We dance to the glory of Bacchus!
We dance to the death of Pentheus,
the dance of the spawn of the dragon!
  He dressed in woman's dress;
  he took the lovely thyrsus;
  it waved him down to death,
  led by a bull to Hades.

The <u>Bacchae</u>

When such deeds are held in honour,
Why should I honour the Gods in the dance?

No longer to the holy place,
to the navel of the earth I'll go
to worship, nor to Abae
nor to Olympia,
unless the oracles are proved to fit,
for all men's hands to point at.

<u>Oedipus the King</u>

Aphrodite! You lead captive
Stubborn hearts of gods and mortals!
At your side with glinting wing
Eros, round his victim swiftly circling,
Hovers over earth and the salt sea's clear song.

<u>Hippolytus</u>[1]

Come to the party. Tragedy is the celebration of disaster.

We sing that we are mortal, that life is right not merely in spite of death but because of it. Yesterday dies that today may be born. Each flash of the present lives at the expense of all time. The softness that makes us frail makes us tender. In our fear lies triumph. In our fury lies love. The grotesque and the

3

sickening are reflexes of desire. The world of the stage--like the stage of the world--is littered with our dead surrounded by the dying. Life is impractical, unfeasible, inconceivable--yet the human animal will take more of it. So, in grim optimism, we congratulate each other: things couldn't be worse. I wish you joy of the worm.

We kill the king because he matters enough. Down with Hamlet, our love and self, and Lear, our dear miserable child-father. If our saviour Oedipus is not destroyed, we will dance no more the holy dance of our drama. The king is our reality and we affirm dithyrambically that it is mortal. Death-bound, we will destroy as we are destroyed and commit the inevitable suicide. But we will go slow and savour the tears, for they belong to us, and we will touch one another in the abandon of sorrow.

We cannot know the meaning of tragedy without losing the knowledge of all that is familiar, stable, and safe, without following Faustus and Macbeth to the prospect of damnation. The mystery seduces us through deep fear, and so it should, for the mystery is our own. It leads toward the love of our own being, awkward and shameful, wrapped in the anguish of self-consciousness, but vibrant and full beyond measure.

The song will carry us if we surrender to it, without cautious thought or superior judgement ("As 'Well, well, we know,' or, 'We could and if we would' . . . "). You may abandon hope who enter here, and all the forms and shapes of sensible control. Without thought and preparation, without beliefs, opinons or judgments, the feelings become clear and reveal their powerful significance.

We proceed with our lives in our hands, and on this sacrifice we ourselves throw incense.

1. Characteristics of Tragedy

A tragedy is a play (in the broader sense of the word, an event) that conveys "the tragic sense of life." The tragic sense of life is a state of mind in which man's situation is experienced as "impossible": inherently self-destructive or dependent on terms that oppose it.

The tragic must be distinguished from the melodramatic and the didactic in drama, from the catastrophic in reality, and from the "merely pathetic" in both.

The tragic sense evokes a complex of feelings organically interrelated: shame, horror, disgust, grief, rage--and the sense of their encompassment. The tragic is always pathetic (arousing pathos) but the pathetic is not always tragic. In the merely pathetic there may be painful sorrow and despair but there is not the immersion in horror that in tragedy evokes a rage of protest, a resistance against the way things are that is one attribute of heroic integrity.

We often say that tragedy is what happens to one or more characters of the play, whom we call the tragic hero or heroes, but more properly tragedy is their condition. If we say it is their fate, then fate is simply the course through which their condition becomes clear to them. Tragedy, most importantly, is what the play communicates. The play is an instrument that functions to make the tragic statement; through their interaction and their self-revelation the characters constitute the play and that statement.[2] The characters function, however, not simply as individuals or as a representative society but as stylized bodies of consciousness. They are figments of feeling, thought, awareness and impact, whose form is controlled by esthetic needs of the play and traditional standards of the culture. As we encounter the play, they unfold their fictive consciousness in our own minds, which encompass their individuality with our esthetic sense of the whole work. Then our feelings consort with one another according to the configurations these characters produce in their own "persons." Tragedy is about the feelings it arouses.

Nevertheless, it is often not enough to say that this play is a tragedy and that is not. Especially when we come to modern drama--from Ibsen on--at times we want to say: this play has a tragic quality, this tends toward the tragic, this is essentially tragic but not manifestly so; and, of course, some of the most important modern works in the tragic mode lie outside drama altogether, such as novels by Faulkner and Hemingway. We should speak sometimes of quasi-tragedy, or "tragedy" in a looser sense, with no disparagement but only a sense of accurate vagueness. Many works partake of the real tragic quality in different ways and to different degrees without being fully immersed in it. They are not <u>not</u> tragic and can be distinguished from spurious tragedies that <u>are</u>.

In spite of our desire to be "fair," tragedy does take on evaluative force. The full tragic statement holds a special place in our consciousness, as an act of intense clarification that requires an honesty of perception and expression. Ordinarily we would insist that there is no goodness in any genre or mode of literature--better a brilliant farce than a mediocre "serious play"--yet a work that is capable of full tragic statement must be a great work. If it is not successful esthetically, it is not really tragic. If it is tragic it achieves stature in spite of any incidental faults.

It is more meaningful to describe characteristics of tragedy than to attempt a definition:

-- <u>the subjective</u>. Tragedy depicts life in the matrix of experience, as a process of feeling, thought, consciousness, interpreting behavior and action through the direct perception of them. It is about living not merely as a human being but as a human <u>self</u>--the universal unique, responsive and affective in a typical but personal way. Tragedy is therefore empirical, affirming knowledge only where it is learned <u>im</u>-mediately-- without the mediation of philosophical speculation or moral presupposition.

-- <u>the definitive</u>. First, tragedy speaks in absolutes, asserting or implying universal truths about the human condition. The tragic complex of feeling is communicated not merely for a character, on behalf of his isolated suffering, but <u>for</u> <u>the</u> <u>way</u> <u>life</u> <u>is</u>. These feelings may not be voiced explicitly within the work itself, by a character, but always they are at least implicit in the qualitative flow of experience that constitutes the dramatic action. Secondly, tragedy cuts through the vague, restrained and continually compromised conditions of ordinary life with a directness and purity of vision that sees the norm in intensity. It encounters evil as absolute evil, agony as absolute agony, and so forth. Its feelings are the epitome of feeling. Its darkness is utter black; its sense of horror disintegrates into nausea.

The generalization of tragedy is not, of course, the objective generalization of induction or consensus, yet it is more than a tentative, hypothetical assertion. It speaks mythically as though it voices all truth in order to chart one absolute dimension of truth. . . . Yet in another sense, no individual work <u>can</u> speak absolutely. The type is not the archetype and to reflect it always alters it. From epoch to epoch, from playwright to playwright, from play to play within one writer's canon, variations bring forth the theme, which cannot be stated otherwise. By being variations, they endow the statement with necessary individuality, immediacy and vitality--but they are variations on a theme and the theme is the essence.

-- <u>the</u> <u>problematic</u>. Tragic life is experienced as a predicament, one that rational or prescriptive interpretation

9

cannot cope with. It is defined by contradiction, paradox, a sense of being trapped in the condition that life be lived under untenable conditions. Though life is impossible, it <u>will</u> be lived. Moreover, it <u>is</u> being lived in the perception that it cannot be lived. . . . The height of tragic knowledge is achieved through the depth of pain and degradation. Life is affirmed through the confrontation with death. Events that should breed pessimism glow with the optimistic warmth of rich emotion. . . . We see tragedy from the perspective of rational expectations, so we are puzzled, shocked and frustrated when the rational mind, confronting organic reality, turns back upon itself in paradox.

-- the <u>violent</u>. The mind both recoils from and protests against the restraints of life in a release of feeling that is destructive of both others and self but that actually expresses a profound desire for life. It is a heroic self-assertion that we respect even amid the carnage. The sensitivity of the mind had been outraged by all the confusion of its integrity that living has brought: the impositions by other people, the distortions of experience by social values, compromises urged by one's own appetites and fears, and the unfairness of all human limitations. In Lear, Hamlet, Othello, or Pentheus, the personality explodes leaving the ashes of madness around it. Such madness is not aberration, however, but life struggling with its own violation.

-- the <u>existential</u>. The mind experiences its absolute impotence in the face of discontinuity, the sense that the terms of existence do not hold together. The mind cannot move from life

10

into death; the individual, unique in the universe, does not seem to belong to the social and conventional environment which presumes to define him. He is torn between: creative potentiality and the continuing norm of frustration; exuberance and the caution for survival; desire and the continually receding horizon of success; memory of past pleasure and realization of present pain; a capacity to live and a compulsion to throttle oneself; simple action and its eddies of consequence. Each of these sources of discontinuity leaves the self acutely aware of its own existence, alone absolutely.

-- the grotesque. At the heart of tragedy, revealed in at least a quick glance, is the disintegration of all decorum into what Conrad's Kurtz calls "the horror." At once repellent and magnetic, it is a nightmare vision that reveals life's "negative space," exploring the forbidden and the imprudent realms of experience, the ugly, the frightening, the vicious, which are all tragic when they come to seem inescapably familiar. The bestial is human, the horrible is natural, chaos is visceral. The esthetic boundaries of the tragedy, which set it off discreetly from the world, may threaten to burst until they are revived on a new level in catharsis.

The tragic hero does not die proudly and neatly on his sword, declaiming a noble farewell. Like Mark Antony, he is more likely to make a mess of it. Othello's final show of pride is desperate, fraught with horrible realization. Critics often distance themselves from the tragic experience by blaming the hero tor

11

immoral behavior (Macbeth is the best example) when they ought to be sharing the terror, shock, and virtual nausea of his confrontation with life.   What is deplorable to morality is grotesque in tragedy, because it is intrinsic, a wound in one's gut. It is not merely inevitable, it is necessary, since it is there: it is now oneself.

   -- the restorative. Tragedy follows a self-validating logic, which derives from a simple proposition: the confrontation with reality is the only source of value. The movement is from an unstable, self-protective condition, through a process of attrition and suffering (ordeal, passion) to a poise of integration, where what has been actively feared is now actively embraced. A new continuity emerges from the experience of discontinuity itself, for the discontinuity is sensed as merely the self's withholding in fear and bewilderment. As the fear dissolves, the center holds its own as it could not do before. The vision of tragedy is eminently organic: ripeness is all.

   Aristotle may have meant that tragedy purges us out of pity and fear through the process he called catharsis or he may have meant that it purges pity and fear of "dangerous" elements. We can use the word to mean what seems more tenable psychologically than either of these possibilities and more true to our actual experience. As we participate imaginatively in the tragic ordeal, we receive under the spell of projection what we ordinarily resist feeling through our identities. Masked, we go forth more securely ourselves. As Hamlet or Othello, we exist

12

tentatively in a stylized life that has--because of its heroic and esthetic sense of elevation---a specialness and an urgency about it. We can then experience as positive the most "negative" emotions. Catharsis, therefore, purges us not out of feelings but into them, and it leads us into our feelings in such a way that we are prepared to accept them and sense them provisionally in a state of poise. What is purged is our resistance, the anxiety or guilt which ordinarily devalues our experience, frustrating and obscuring it.

Even such painful modern works as Endgame and The Chairs remain life-giving and we pay to see them. They restore us to the reality of our feelings, affirming our experience as experience, no matter how grotesque or morally problematic it may be, if the feelings are honestly conveyed. We may remain terribly disturbed; we may leave the theater with more of a consciousness of pain that was only latent before, but we sense a legitimacy to the disturbance, perhaps even (in the courage of our negativism) with a certain satisfaction that overshoots the mark and leaves us a bit complacent with our fortitude. . . . Catharsis is that factor which makes the spectacle of misery a positive experience.

* * * * *

"Tragedy" can be studied fruitfully as the history of a word, one that links a vaguely associated cluster of notions. We can study what the term has meant in different epochs or what it means to us now when we apply it to authors as distant from each other as Racine and Dostoyevsky. On the other hand, tragedy can be studied as a phenomenon, in both the ordinary and the philosophical sense, if we are willing to let the word serve to point towards that phenomenon. If we are willing to assume, also, that art is an extension of immediate reality and must be understood through the consciousness that infuses it (and that criticism is a way of evoking that consciousness in itself)--then we can study art for the life in it.

We might also assume--a notion that some readers may not deem intellectually responsible--that there is a reality which can be known, a tendency of common human experience.

Tragedy conveys a sense of reality that is somewhat elusive yet quite consistent. If we heed its rhythms, we see that the plays are extremely emphatic about what that reality is like. We must risk the possibility, however, that this kind of meaning is to be known not through logical speculation nor through consensus popular or elite nor through objective demonstration. It is to be known through a consciousness of ourselves in relation to the plays--subjectively though not impressionistically, personally though not privately, emotionally though not un-intellectually. The risk of error is considerable, yet it is not the relativistic limitation of intellectual theory, asserting that every opinion has an absolute validity from its arbitrary viewpoint. The risk is the inevitable (tragic?) confusion and dimness of our own unconsciousness--but that is exactly what we are reflecting upon. If we wish to dive in, at any rate, the right direction will certainly be downward.

14

2. Tragic Reality

"I suppose this reads like 'Oedipus
Rex' or something out of a soap opera,
but it's actually a tragedy," said one
of the attorneys for a mother and son
who married each other and have pleaded
guilty to bigamy.
San Jose Mercury, Sept. 4, 1971

In order to speculate flexibly, we can assert three partly contradictory truths that overlap: tragedy is a dimension of life, tragedy is an esthetic event, tragedy is a phase of consciousness.

To say that life is tragic is to say that the horrible is an inherent, natural aspect of being. There is a casual normality to be faced in what is outrageously unfair, self-defeating, violent. Ordinarily, we cannot help but depend upon others who are hostile or indifferent to our interests, with whom we continually negotiate frustrating compromises. In order to live we submit to an organic gravity that leads us all down through the logic of pain to the eventual grave in spite of bootstrap-tugging, that sucks

15

anonymous masses down into historic cataclysms or "acts of God."
There is natural tragedy in the rhythm that brings time after time
a backlash of distress for each advantage, that reveals with every
good or gain the underside of some loss that it depends upon.

> Pity would be no more
> If we did not make somebody Poor . . .

Most spectacularly, the rhythm seems typified in the ultimate
drift of our tragic culture, in the confusion of emotions and of
values that has come along inevitably with the achievements of
our sensible materialism, so that we would become capable of
destroying the world just when we might be alienated enough to
let ourselves do it.[3]

We can indeed say objectively that life is tragic in this sense
so long as we are saying it is a fact that human life is subjective.
We mean then it is tragic that man is conscious of his problematic
situation, that he is capable of a sense of horror in a world which
is up to far more than his worst expectations. One can go even
further. Heinrich Zimmer (who escaped Nazi Germany) writes in
striking terms: "Life is much too horrible in its inescapable,
unmerited and unjustified possibilities of sorrow to be termed
'tragic.' The 'tragic' view is, so to say, only a foreground view,
held by people who marvel still, unable to conceive that life is the
thing it is."[4] It must be an understatement to say that life is
unfair, on the basis of ordinary assumptions, or that it is fraught
with senseless brutality. Ineradicable and frequently desperate
unconsciousness is and always will be the norm out of which

16

people must function as best they can--the others we are dependent upon and ourselves as well--and the spectacle is not inherently gratifying.

We should distinguish between saying that life is tragic and saying that tragedies occur in life. The disasters reported by the headlines are tragic to those involved, but tragedy is the last effect that will be conveyed through the excitation of journalism. There is even a tragic discontinuity between the headlines and the experience of those stricken. Accidents do not become more tragic with each auto added to the pile-up, of course; each person's experience is complete in itself and corpses, presumably, have no experience at all. One can realize one's own prospective annihilation as tragic, and a survivor can sense his loss as tragic. An event like a political assassination can feel tragic if one relates to the public figure through a mythic identification, in which case the experience is close to a literary one. One can feel a tragic outgoing toward a passerby on the street or a fellow passenger on a train. But in all possibilities, the tragic dimension depends upon a feeling about one's own life. What necessary hope has been extinguished? What promise of fulfillment has been withdrawn?

> It ís the blight man was born for,
> It is Margaret you mourn for.

To say that life is worse than tragic is to suggest that the sense of dignity and poise we expect of tragedy is appropriate only to tragic art, where the esthetic qualities of formal structure,

17

eloquence of language, stylization of character and perspicuity of insight elevate the perceiver into a state of grace. So we reach the sense in which tragedy is an esthetic event. We should consider the possibility, however, that the esthetic form merely symbolizes the wholeness and smoothness of feeling always potential in reality though rarely fulfilled. What the grace of art imitates, then, is the ideal flow of direct living, anticipating a fulfillment that still hovers in abeyance.

The third level of truth, standing between the other two, requires special emphasis, and most of what follows in these notes will be an attempt to clarify it: tragedy is a phase of consciousness; as a literary form it is an imitation of that phase. In life facts are tragic by perception, in literature by treatment. An assertion about life from the tragic perspective is just that, an assertion from the tragic perspective, a self-substantiating mood.

Comedy and tragedy both express the rhythm of the essential psychic archetype: the structure of experience in which consciousness encounters the threat of chaos or death and encompasses it. As Northrop Frye writes, "tragedy is really implicit or uncompleted comedy" while "comedy contains a potential tragedy within itself."[5] Myth provides the overall scenario, the skeleton of the unitary tragicomedy--the Ur-story of death and rebirth--while drama, sophisticating the mode of ritual, fleshes out the skeleton, providing body and substance to the structure. The mind's feelings are focussed and conveyed through stylistic projection--tragedy stylizing its reality on the basis of

18

horror and resistance, comedy on the basis of integration and joy. Joseph Campbell writes: "Tragedy is the shattering of the forms and of our attachment to the forms; comedy, the wild and careless, inexhaustible joy of life invincible."[6] Each perspective, however, suggests the same rhythm: any length of arc carries the same curve.

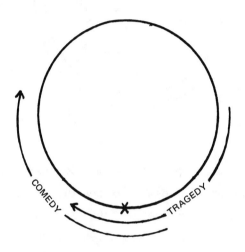

The structure of the psyche _is_ the interrelationship between the conscious mind and the unconscious. It is useful to see this total relationship in three phases: 1) the rational, superficially conscious mind, the ego, with which we identify ourselves in our unconsciousness; 2) tragic consciousness, in which we experience the painful vision feared by the self-protective ego; and 3) true consciousness, the potentiality of fulfillment through the integration of what we have feared.

19

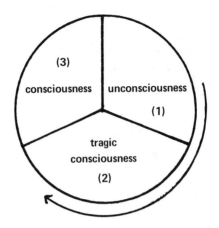

Tragedy, then, is the perspective on unconscious horror seen from the restricted consciousness. To say that it is a "phase of consciousness" now means that it is the reluctant movement from the first phase to the second with a sense of the third suggested ahead. In these terms we expect the tragic hero to be so weighty (have such "magnitude") that he will fall heavily enough to find a momentum up the curve. He may suggest this ascent in self-realization before he dies, or the very thoroughness of his experience may suggest it, or it may be implicit in the tone and tenor of the play around him. Obviously, therefore, the play cannot be said to <u>have a tragic ending</u>. The hero's ordeal clarifies what has always been true and the play is tragic at every moment: from the opening fraught with dreadful potentiality, through every stage of its unravelling, beyond the absolutes of chaos to the poise on the other side.

A work may have the form of tragedy in its plot and even in its implications without a tragic texture of feeling. On the other hand, it may deal with tragic knowledge in a manner that is not tragic, because it approaches the vision retrospectively perhaps, from the perspective of integration. This can be said of many Greek plays that have "happy endings," like The Eumenides, Alcestis and Philoctetes. It can also be said of Arthur Miller's After the Fall and the modern "tragedies of sainthood," even therefore of Passion plays. These are all plays about catharsis rather than cathartic plays. They are celebrations of catharsis rather than disaster, representing the extension of tragedy that overlaps on romance. Christianity itself can be seen in this light, a fulfillment and not a negation of tragedy, if it is taken as myth rather than doctrine. As much Christian art testifies, the agony of the Passion must seem absolute if salvation is to have meaning. Hence Christ's last cry.

Romance is the tendency of comedy to absorb tragedy. In moments of "comic relief" and absurdist grotesquerie we usually see tragedy's tendency to absorb comedy, for while we laugh at the Porter in Macbeth or the witful naivete of Beckett's tramps, the chasm widens at our feet. The laughter does not turn hollow exactly; what seems funny is funny, but it is all the more pathetic for not being sentimentalized away. The validity of a detached perspective intensifies our aloneness. It comes to seem painful that we can laugh at such matters. It comes to seem tragic that

21

life is comic. The measure of a tragicomic balance is how we feel when the laughter subsides, and if the two emotional tones are simply placed side-by-side, without a stylized preparation for romance, the "heavier" is likely to be the more convincing.

It is possible, however, for humor and pathos to stand together in a kind of exceptional purity, a complementarity in which neither comments on the other while both create a greater whole. In the medieval mystery plays innocent frolic makes its own contribution to the plays' reverence for all life. Perhaps Shakespeare's most exalted moments are the appearances of humble old fumblers like Dogberry and Verges, Shallow and Silence. In them the ridiculous and the sublime are one and the same, a perfect and awesome life-feeling of delight in sorrow and a joyful dignity in the perception of weakness.

Seeing tragedy as a phase should imply the important dimension of it that is process and hence the importance of drama as the standard means of portraying it. Many poems express or approach a tragic tonality and various works of fiction are tragic in quality, conveying the tragic sense. Yet we speak only of certain plays as being in themselves "tragedies," and there may be some good reason for doing so. The temporal structure of drama, the play's existence in an evolving present, helps to materialize the tragedy as a revelation, for tragic drama is an occurring mode of perception rather than a static picture. It occurs through a resistance to its perception (the exercise of hybris), the collapse of resistance in the impotence of discovery, and the growth of a poise beyond vulnerability as the pain is integrated in catharsis. The resistance, the discovery and the integration all have their meaning only in terms of one another, pain taking the measure of prosperity and prosperity of pain.

While the tragic work is seen unfolding significantly in time, it is also seen as a whole statement. In this view the tragic perspective is seen to move simultaneously in two directions: from unconsciousness or hybris forward into the nightmare and from cathartic poise backward to the chaos it envelopes and preserves. Each viewpoint relates to the other as an absolute. The prospect of dissolution must be asserted and dramatized as the utter truth of death, tangibly factual and irremediable. But without losing this feeling--catharsis does not change life, only our relationship to it--we get the contrary inclusive view, that the worst pain and horror can be integrated and sensed in a new way, both fair and just and even desirable.

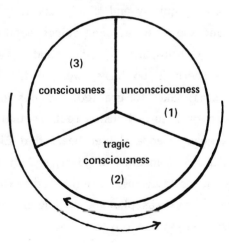

All tragedies say essentially the same thing: life is tragic. It is the quality of feeling that makes a play tragic, the integrity of insight--not the extent of the circle it covers but the accuracy of the curve and the direction it leads. The dissolution of Mrs. Alving's reality at the end of Ghosts is the real thing, and flights of angels could add nothing substantial that is not already implied. Only a moment is required--the last in the play--to strike the appropriate chord, though the rest of the play prepares for it, building the structure that is to collapse.

In most tragedies there is such a moment of negative epiphany when the hero's world dissolves. It is, of course, the recognition scene, anagnorisis, which registers the impact of tragic realization on the dramatized consciousness of a self. Everything else in the play is at the service of this moment, leading up to it and then levelling off. When it is to come, the audience is alert, ahead of the hero, waiting for the kill. The moment usually comes quietly and simply, for it is the ultimate understatement and the hero has been going ahead busily in the opposite direction. One listens: amid the sound and fury occurs a ringing silence. There is no basis, we see the hero see, to everything that he has taken for granted. Oedipus learns he was a babe of the house of Laius. Faustus realizes that when death comes, it comes now. Hedda Gabler hears that Eilert Lövborg died of a wound in his stomach. Strindberg's Captain hears that his wife actually means to dispose of him. Mother Courage learns that her son, whom she was planning to buy off from a firing squad, has thrown the cash box into the river.

24

This moment of recognition is more important than anything that may follow it at the end of the play and it is more important than any specific attributes of the hero's personality. The devastation it effects cannot be erased or obscured once the play has recorded it, and it at once reduces personality and all cultural influences to a common level of minor relevance. The one essential attribute of the tragic hero is that he have the capacity to register this recognition, even though he may do so quite tacitly and in spite of himself, and this capacity consists of the hybris to resist that knowledge which is to be revealed.

There is an important desire, expressed by some critics and by some playwrights, to assert that true tragedy is not cathartic at all, because catharsis must be a benign coverup of grim reality, an apparent solution to what cannot be solved. Toward the same end Brecht and his followers reject tragedy because it is cathartic. Tragedy, however, does say that life is "worse than tragic." When we feel that the truth is too overwhelming to be embraced, then tragedy renews itself with vivid immediacy. When we read in the newspaper about nightmares humans perpetrate on one another, literary tragedy seems pale and the word "tragedy" an insult upon enormous injury. We see photographs of war victims or even a painting like "Guernica" and we are struck with nausea, rage and a pathos that is as far beyond "pity" as death is beyond the poets' "sleep." We are furious at the men of letters, like Tom Stoppard's Rosencrantz and Guildenstern thrashing the actor who merely plays a death scene. Then we want to say: this, reality, is really tragic--and the word is reborn on a new level of consciousness. And we may remember how the same feeling came to us in reading Lear or The Bacchae.

At this point we touch the nadir of the tragic process, the depth of chaos. Classical plays may pass through it quickly, modern plays often dwell upon it. Thus some plays of the absurd--plays of Ionesco, Beckett and Pinter--stress the static quality of being caught in the nightmare so strongly that they show nothing else. Their movement along the curve is minimal and critics have argued whether they in particular carry any catharsis. These plays are often tragic, whatever else they may be as well, because the quality of feeling they project has the solidity of the tragic sense. They clarify the most important part of the circle, the dead bottom, adding depth where traditional tragedy surpasses in breadth. The second phase is given the absolute expression it really needs to be accurate--the horrible with no mitigation. The first phase we bring to the confrontation ourselves. The third comes from our capacity to accept what is offered. We are schooled in this, as we are in any tragedy, by the tone of the play--the fortitude of its presentation.

Tragedy is hard to define because once it is understood it is no longer in the same sense tragic, for hero, for audience, or for critic. Jaspers distinguishes between "deliverance achieved within the tragic, and deliverance from the tragic":

> Either the tragic remains intact, and man liberates himself by enduring it and transforming himself within

26

it, or else tragedy itself is, so to speak, redeemed; it ceases to be; it becomes past. Man had to journey through it, but what was tragic has now been penetrated, abolished on its old level; yet fundamentally it is preserved and made the foundation of real life which is now no longer tragic.[7]

To clarify tragedy we spiral above it again and again. The problem looks different from the point of view of resistance and that of acceptance. The tragic phase passes into the divine-comic in ecstasy, smilingly, " 'Twixt two extremes of passion, joy and grief . . ." It is fortunate, of course, that the hero's protest is doomed to failure, for his surrender yields a reality that is new though always the same, fresh and hopeful though uncompromisingly severe. We return to our ordinary state of frustration with some new or renewed confidence that there is a place for it in the scheme of things. Confusion and violence and fear belong organically to the whole, a fact that can be seen best through blindness in the heart of darkness.

The metaphysical significance of myth (and hence of tragedy) lies merely in its rhythm of dissolution and confirmation. This rhythm itself identifies a clarity that subsumes the dualisms between the one and the many, the self and the other, individualism and adjustment, life and death, consciousness and unconsciousness--and the dualism, most basically, between dualism and monism. The circle, as in the uroboros, is the inevitable result of a linear process at once defeating and fulfilling its nature. It no longer goes anywhere and it goes everywhere. It is formal and it is infinite. It opens and turns back

27

on itself. "We are all our lifetime reading the copious sense of this first of forms," writes Emerson in the essay called "Circles." Freed from spatial ratio, every point is the circle of the universe. Antony and Cleopatra are married in Egyptian-Roman-Elizabethan heaven, Act VI, eternity. Wherever we think we are, we are everywhere, for each point on the circle implies the whole. Our truth is mortal truth; divinity, however, emerges through our tragic form and catharsis is its name.

3. Tragedy and Guilt

It has been argued, in a humane spirit, that tragedy portrays the suffering of guilty men who take responsibility for their guilt in contrast to (mere) pathos or melodrama, which portrays the unjustified suffering of the innocent. Only action, the dynamic, is tragic; a state of being, the passive, is at most pathetic.[8]

It may be said, to take a different tack, that there are two tragedies in life: one that we are guilty and the other that we are innocent--or more precisely--a) it is tragic that we cannot live without guilt[9] and b) it is tragic that we must die in spite of our innocence. In both cases the "moral" qualities, guilt and innocence, are absolute. It is important that in a the guilt is relevant as a quality of living, not as a cause of dying. The guilt is a general burden experienced personally rather than any specific arbitrary fault or "tragic flaw." In b, the second sense of tragedy, innocence is not celebrated as a quality of life (goodie for Little Nell) but is offered violently in protest against life's failure to explain death.

$\underline{A}$ produces the classical tragedy of moral responsibility, of which Macbeth and Oedipus are exemplars of different types; $\underline{b}$ produces existential tragedy of protest, Hamlet being primarily of this class though it bridges the gap. Hamlet pursues the consciousness of existence and of guilt in terms of each other. The Book of Job is a clearer example of $\underline{b}$. In the Hippolytus, Phaedra is a character exemplar of $\underline{a}$, Hippolytus of $\underline{b}$, Theseus bridging the gap. Having brought together the son and the second-wife, and having judged them falsely in defense of dignity and domesticity, Theseus is responsible for what happens to them both. At the end, he is left alive with a consciousness that embraces their double ordeal. The Apollonian Artemis of Hippolytus and the Dionysian Aphrodite working through Phaedra come together perhaps in Theseus' father Poseidon, god of a venerable symbol for the unconscious mind. (Both Hamlet and Lear have been said to derive from sea gods!)

Typically in a tragedy, an inevitability of guilt derives from some particular emotion which must destroy others in order to realize itself. The hero endures the blooming of his passion together with the free growth of its implications. There is nauseous horror at the realization of his own capacity for atrocity, which seems absolute. His crime makes him monstrous. As the tragic process unfolds, however, what is felt as guilt transcends into responsibility, which is the recognition of implications. As the fact of the crime dissolves in consciousness, the odium attached to it recedes.

Beyond the character's personal situation, tragic guilt records what is horrendous in humanly organic nature. We take our pleasures in the face of others' pain, we accept our life in the consciousness of others' death. We take whatever the world can give us, killing perpetually for our survival: in the thoughts and feelings that slay even without expression, in the myriad forms of personal manipulation, in the stifling of our own better selves--as well as in our abandonment of millions of people to starvation, our elimination of inconvenient criminals, our slaughter of enemies. There must be food for the body, food for the ego, and food for all the drives that press us onward. Though the abyss of guilt is a dreadful prospect, we are desperately committed to it and must acknowledge it as our home.

But on the other hand, as we face the abyss of death, no degree of remorse or sensitivity can matter. Justice, gratification, knowledge, the accumulation of experience-- everything that should help to balance the scale evaporates as our all becomes as if it never were. Nothing compensates for anything else. There is no proportion, no relationship. Because death is absolute as a consequence of living, man, when he recognizes his death, is absolute in his integrity. Whatever he does, in fact, reflects his struggle to cope with impossible circumstances. And if he lives according to his sensitivity, with idealistic discipline, the tragedy of his existence will be even more apparent, since his dependence upon the terms of life will seem all the more irrelevant.

What makes b (existence) tragic as well as a (guilt) is the disparity--the outrageous lack of continuity between cause and effect--which in either case leaves one exposed to the profound revelation of his inevitable impotence, the absolute limitation of the will he must assert to attempt control of his situation and the absolute uselessness of his conscious, rational mind to produce an understanding that will give him control. The discontinuity itself leaves us dumbstruck, with the sense that life cannot possibly work. No rational orientation will be relevant now and there can be no compromise.

Just as we cannot be ourselves without guilt (a), so we cannot possibly be guilty enough to die (b). No act, nothing so specific and limited, can explain the totality of present felt pain, let alone the prospect of annihilation. And at this point we may sense that, though writers, cultures or plays may stress one or the other, the two tragedies (a and b) are really one, the essential paradox of mortality: that organic existence is dying life and that death is not merely non-existence but a function of being. The process that kills is the same that makes us killers. We deal in death because we die.

There is another way in which the two tragedies become one. Hamlet and Hippolytus are tragic because they are destroyed by life, or to put it in other words, they exemplify the fact that life itself is tragic, destroying because it is organic. They are existentially tragic, but at the same time they are, like the more-or-less Shakespearean Pericles, guilty of trying to be innocent.

32

And they are guilty of being innocent even though innocent is, by definition, precisely what they should be. That is another way of saying they are guilty of being alive, in the human condition.

In the romance, Pericles must and should flee the repulsive, destructive exploitation by adulterous father and daughter. Just the same, he is responsible for shunning a human phenomenon, as monstrous as it is, and his sufferings are the appropriate working out of a resonsibility he must bear. He is as bound by the incest of others that he flees as Oedipus is bound by the incest he commits unintentionally. Zimmer writes,

> Those who are innocent always strive to exclude from themselves and to negate in the world the possibilities of evil. This is the reason for the persistence of evil-- and this is evil's secret.[10]

Hippolytus offends against an equally monstrous Aphrodite and though he too remains innocent, he remains responsible. For the monstrous is also human, and the offense remains an offense. Tragically, innocence is not enough even though it is perfect. The innocent, in fact, have a special responsibility of their own that is particularly awful, particularly tragic. It adds to their stature by denying then the solace of moral simplicity.

Tragedy, then, can be explained as the painful apprehension of unqualified human vulnerability (mortality) confronted through the natural passion to accrue powers and experience, effectiveness and gratification (hybris), to actively and willfully

33

live. The passion to live makes the full difficulty of living seem horrible. The sense of life's severity makes the idealistic wishfullness and intense sensibility seem boldly heroic. It is probably most accurate to say that the tragic emotion lies in the tension itself, this tension of enormous sadness between the heroic and the horrible, the richness and the barrenness, the innocence of poignant desire and the wretchedness of stupid, violent helplessness.

In contrast to tragedy, melodrama is likely to be rational and morally gratifying. The punishment will fit the crime. The pathetic and the moralistic modes both fall short of the tragic though they may simulate b (the tragedy of existence), the pathetic sensing death but remaining weakly paralyzed by the fear of it; the moralistic erecting a structure of righteousness, honor or stoic pride to repel the full consciousness of horror. "Neo-classical tragedy," a contradiction in terms, disapproves of the emotionalism it exploits or else embraces it with the facility of incomprehension. In either case it remains alienated from its emotional center, no matter how intensely or articulately the passion may be expressed.

Thus Racine's Phèdre is a play of the hatred of passion rather than of passion itself. It is fraught with a sense of life's darkness, but though the darkness is magnetic, it is not enlivening; it is not paradoxical. This is emphasized by the contrast of Hippolyte and Aricie's wholesome love and admirable conduct with what is continually felt by the heroine and everybody else except

34

the clearly deplorable Oenone as sickness and crime. If there is any tragic consciousness in the play, it must come through the perspective of Thesée at the very end, as it does in Euripides, yet this is clearly not the drift of the play.

4. Hybris and the Unconscious

The burden of tragedy is the experience--the subjective knowledge--of mortality: the condition of being organic and hence death-bound (bound towards death as destination and bound by it as a continual condition); subject to contingency, time and space, identity (existing as one's self), and the very un-godlike disjunction between desire and fulfillment that constitutes work; and suspended in a condition of basic being not continuous with any moral or speculative perspective that may offer objective coherence. In this sense, tragedy can be called an experiential definition of the human condition. To be human is to be mortal; to be mortal is to be vulnerable, open to pain, dissolution, and the ordeal of shame. But to know what all this means humanly implies discovering it and feeling it through one's own being, and no level of theory, no other values, must circumvent this subjective learning and relearning.

The method of tragedy lies through confrontation between the restricted, self-protective state of consciousness, within which we ordinarily live, and the open, painful state of consciousness that we habitually ward off. The confrontation unfolds the potentialities of consciousness in one process of passion. Dramatic action dramatizes this confrontation (makes it happen) and the transition from the closed state to the open that must grow out of an honest challenge. What is dramatic, we say, is conflict and process: learning, that is, through happening. The confrontation may occur explicitly through the agon between representative characters, but it may occur simply between the (external) perspective of the audience and the (internal) dislocation of ordinary assumptions that the play's passion dramatizes.

Hybris is defined traditionally as the "overweening pride" with which a mortal assumes the prerogatives of deity. It can be seen more clearly and less moralistically as that "normal" condition of unconsciousness through which most of us manage our lives--or, more emphatically, that condition when its claims are pressed with heroic integrity. The cautious chorus may be equally unconscious but it serves typically as the background out of which tragic man emerges. He insists with violent integrity that life must be dealt with through the natural and only means at his disposal: the understanding, passion and will which are in the broad view imperfect but which are the given terms in the frustrated condition of ordinary reality. This condition is in fact the starting point from which we--and the chorus standing out from us and the personae standing out from the chorus--must encounter the revelation.

37

The hero's hybris cannot be seen fairly as a "flaw" as long as that term has a judgmental--and therefore alienating--force.[11] The hero had the sensitivity to fear life as it really is, to be repelled by its sordidness in favor of a constructive idealism. But he becomes at some point clearly as grotesque as what he fears. The nightmare, naturally, is himself. Hamlet's rectitude is a disgust with life that contorts his own features as his knowledge of life ripens into decay. Oedipus the king is also the outcast; the judge is the condemned man, the hunter the prey, the curser the accursed. On the tragic level, it is always the detective who has done it.

The hybris of Oedipus is his self-deception that the two sides of his nature, his innocence and his guilt, can be separated. It is his unconsciousness of the paradox waiting to trap him as long as he insists that his real identity can be directed through action and through choice. Ordinarily, we all live this way, along the linear pursuits of goals and gratifications made possible by myriad vague compromises, avoidances, surrenders, by arbitrary assumptions or "beliefs" that are from one point of view really quite desirable. They have their inevitability, their necessity. Our further questions are raised hesitantly, speculatively, effecting us only so far as they may be needed to solve practical conflicts or justify decisions already made in our hearts.

By pressing his questions, the hero reaches a point where he is no longer practically, politically (according to the symbolism of drama) useful, like both Lear and Hamlet in their different tragic

38

ways, and Prospero in the way of romance. What makes the hero essentially different from us in tragedy is not that he simply makes a mistake nor should it have been that he has made a wise decision. It is, rather, appropriately, the quality of single-mindedness, the integrity, with which he insists upon our desirable fallacies.

The hero, thus, tests out for us to the limit the assumptions by which we live, sacrificing himself to their logic. Macbeth's hybris works out a paradigm of social ambition to its natural conclusion. Hamlet's hybris takes the form of a righteous bitterness that is fully justified at the same time that it is ultimately quite irrelevant. In either instance and in all others that are properly tragic, the hero acts as he must and should act given the fact that, like us all, he is merely human--driven, that is, against the form of his own humanity.

That such a one as this is caught in our own plight adds conviction and dignity to our humble difficulties. It induces us to respect ourselves. (In "The Defense of Poetry," Shelley points out that "drama of the highest order" teaches self-respect as well as self-knowledge.) On the other hand, it also evokes from us a kind of commitment toward the hero. As he accepts responsibility for our condition, so we share a responsibility for his fate. We are involved in the hero because he expresses us. He has a stature, therefore, because of his hybris, because of his basic fallacies, and of course, he has a complementary stature on a grander order because he seems to pass beyond us and our illusions. By pressing

39

our assumptions to the limit, he explodes them. Yet this truly heroic stature belongs to us too in a way, for it projects the fulfillment of our potentialities.

The moral rationalist thinks it is deplorably tragic that the hero yields to his hybris or is mastered by it. Through our own commitment to hybris we realize it is otherwise. It is tragic that hybris is doomed, that unconsciousness cannot work, while all we know how to want is the gratification of our unconsciousness. It seems that fumbling in the dark is all that life will afford us and it seems to be all we dare attempt. We are bound to feel that life must materialize in terms we can really grasp and these terms are bound to be the terms rooted in the despair clinging to security.

Yet, in the long run, in the overview, how fortunate it is that this state of self-frustration can expend itself into some release. How lucky, furthermore, that we are entitled to sense our potential achievement through our own familiar frustrations as they explode into the clarity of catharsis. The necessity of our fears is recognized at the same time that it is relieved. We are rounding again the full circle of mortal paradox: how fortunate that life is tragic. It works only because it is horrible.

What is tragic is that Oedipus cannot avoid the oracle, that Lear cannot crawl unburdened toward his death, that Faustus cannot gain the infinite power we all ordinarily thirst for, that Hedda Gabler cannot create a world of beauty out of her bitterness. We get the fully tragic impact when we feel that they

40

should be able to do so. If only they could! It is tragic that Macbeth cannot kill his king with impunity. Only after that is clarified can we appreciate the further truth: we must prefer that life be tragic--as if we had any choice in the matter. The alternatives are more horrendous.

And to peel one more skin of the onion: the deadly comfort of the hero's fallacies will reconcile us to the fate we share with him. It is only because we have endorsed Mrs. Alving's humane liberalism, feeling it life-supporting, that we can accept the mission she must face at the end of Ghosts. She is qualified to perform the horrible act because she is horrified by it, even because she herself is going to be destroyed by it.

Hybris is an inadequate vision in the long run, but the long run can be achieved only through the short run. Hybris asserts a limited truth, that man can make of his life what he wishes. But the full truth is that he is limited. This he must learn by being limited as perversely as he possibly can. The path, being circular, must head in the wrong direction. Hybris is error but positive error, committed on our behalf in a cause we must respect towards an end we secretly desire but despair of.

The hero plunges headlong into his fallacy, yet in taking the plunge he is way ahead of the rest of us, who hold behind with the chorus, conferring on ethics and expedience. If the hero's hybris leads where angels fear to tread, the loss, from the tragic point of view, is the angels', since man's grace rests upon his vulnerability.

41

Hamlet's pained protest cries that life must not be the proliferation of decadence and decay, though the tragic truth towards which the Ghost points suggests that it is. Who will not support Hamlet in this hybris? And who will not himself feel pained that such protest is self-deception, a voice of what both should and must be rather than of what is?

Oedipus is hybristic when as Able-man he confirms the human domain of civilization through the flowering of his cunning, and again when he defends the basis of all civilization in his promise: I the king will save you, my people, from him, that one, who brings disaster. He is hybristic when he tries to do "the decent human thing" and block the oracle. He could not humanly seek simply to fulfill the oracle, to commit his atrocities deliberately, nor could he live indifferent to the oracle, not caring or fearing or recoiling in horror. If he does come to terms with horror it is, as it must be, only after seeing it as horror, after first fearing it and than feeling its pain. Nor, of course, could he succeed in the absurd effort to avoid the oracle, for oracle and destiny are by definition true and inevitable. Euripides courts melodrama in his Electra when he rather awkwardly doubts this.

Hugo von Hofmannsthal's beautiful play Oedipus and the Sphinx centers on the paradox that Laius' abandonment of his infant son was a "sacrifice to life" on the father's behalf. Laius was destroyed because he chose to live. His rejected son and the Sphinx emerge retributively as two sides of the death he has attempted to avoid, until Oedipus inevitably repeats his father's "mistake" by challenging the Sphinx and then taking Jocasta as his bride.[12] Thus the only "tragic flaw" is our disinclination that life be dreadful: it is mortal that we wish not to be mortal (to affect deity). Mortality is, to be sure, a limitation, but tragedy challenges us--virtually dares us--to continue regarding our humanity as a flaw. It shames us away from the choric expediences that reduce the paradoxes of tragic life to simplistic and melodramatic formulas.

* * * * *

A special form of tragic hybris appears in a mid-genre, tragic satire. The satirist's insight lends him a fierce pride of heroic stature. When he lampoons fashions and institutions, he is a reformer everyone is eager to join. When his mockery challenges some common tricks of human nature, however, absurd quirks that we depend upon in our ordinary vulnerability, he leads us into the more dangerous frontiers of satire. If his position is pressed to its conclusion with the integrity that the satirist's role always implies, he must face a tragic obligation to reject life itself.

Having successfully demolished mankind, the satirist remains in lofty isolation, a cranky Gulliver with no basis for his own humanity. His honesty and insight have made it impossible for him to live. Gulliver is no more "wrong" than any tragic hero nor is the extremity of his final position merely excess. If one claims the benefits of the first three books he must pay the price of the fourth. It merely projects the unconscious underside of their substantial enlightenment. If the result is a critique of pure reason, as many critics now assert, it is as much a protest against the conditions of life which make a reasonable existence impracticable.

As W.B.C. Watkins has shown, tragic satire, not the "heroic" drama, is the true tragedy of the neo-classicists.[13] The casual speech of Dr. Johnson affirms this and Book IV of The Dunciad with its awesome parody of Genesis. Alceste represents the satirist's ultimate predicament in The Misanthrope, although the play itself balances his perspective both with his own self-satire and with the good natured humor of Philinte, this last tone prevailing. There is a significant hint of a tragic undercurrent beneath the sophistication of The Way of the World:

> . . . one's cruelty is one's power; and when one parts with one's cruelty, one parts with one's power; and when one has parted with that, I fancy one's old and ugly.

One is trapped by one's own delight in a civilization of necessary lies, but further by one's own awareness of the trap, which releases, so delicately, a frisson of desperation.

Hamlet, the character, speaks typically as tragic satirist, lacerating himself and the world at the same time, but the major dramatic work itself in this vein is Troilus and Cressida. Here the only possible response to the understanding of one's own

44

commitments is the self-destroying rage of either an obscene Thersites or a berserk Troilus, two sides of the same fallen hybris.

In modern times satiric tragedy is a major mode of expression in all literary forms but it has been most conspicuous in the drama. It is the characteristic tone of the absurdists. One can argue for it in the whimsical-philosophical drama of the French. It figures strongly in plays of Brecht, where the brutalizing of esthetic sensibilities comes to mimic the brutality of life itself. In The Wild Duck heroic integrity is satirized somewhat in the manner of The Misanthrope but with a vicious grotesqueness. Modern man typically seems so self-conscious about his desire for dignity that he must lash it out himself. Satire lends itself naturally to the expression of his shame. He punishes himself with intelligence, twisting himself back into the self-hatred that has had him trapped all along. He begins, in fact, where Oedipus ends, the admitted victim of his own curse.

5. Will and the Tragic Destiny

It is true both that the hero chooses (the ordeal of facing his choice may constitute a major part of the plot) and that his catastrophe is inevitable. It is inevitable not merely from his choice but from his nature--his nature personally and what underlies his personality, his nature as a hero. Tragic inevitability, and the sense of doom that it implies, belongs to the structure of tragedy, and it shows how plot, characterization, mood and "theme" are all responses to the same drive in the sense of life that they convey. A consciousness of doom or of ugly danger is begun by the first lines in high tragedy (Othello is a good example); it does not cause the action, yet the drama as a whole seems to grow out of it. Oracles, ghosts, witches and soothsayers give the fictional impression that they are controlling agents but they are essentially structural manifestations of the mood, which in itself is the main burden of the drama.

In the tragic context, the dualism between free will and determinism is seen as an intellectual fallacy, paranoid perhaps (What, me not free?), and implicitly hybristic. As a man the hero is _free_, at best, only to press his hybris (or not). However, the structure of consciousness determines that hybris must fail to encompass the human problem. The hero's destiny is his potentiality for consciousness (the potentiality always implicit in unconsciousness). He is free to accept what consciousness reveals by necessity, but of course he is not free to choose what it will reveal. He is free to reject what it reveals, once the revelation begins to manifest itself, only through self-deception, which is no real freedom at all. What is determined and what is revealed is that man is mortal. Such symbolic figures as Apollo (in Oedipus, manifesting truth) and Dionysos or Aphrodite (in The Bacchae and Hippolytus respectively, both embodying life force) confront the hero with a realization of the way things are, the "rules of the game," and these are the terms of mortality which he cannot help but live by.

As a fictive person, the hero is designed to choose the road to (creative) ruin. At the same time, as a symbol, he is designed to express a tendency of life to gravitate towards a tragic norm. In a sense, then, he is a hero because he cannot avoid acceptance; he _is_ the course of integrity, which simply registers what should be self-evident, because he will "know not 'seems'." It is the hero's passion to be so, to passively let reality happen to him, thus partaking of its absolute activity. Being "only human" (hybristic) he will not be passive without protest, nor would he be sympathetic (really human) if he were. His _passion_, therefore, a reduction of the will to destiny, is passivity under protest. The truth must not be true, he cries, reflecting the enormity of the

47

truth in the magnitude of his resistance to it.

Unconsciousness perpetuates itself, the restricted mind resisting reality with all the aggression that has made the truth unconscious in the first place. The hybristic hero resists knowledge of himself with a power as mighty as his ignorance. Pentheus is the best example of this, his determined statesmanship being in the end only the measure of his seeping prurience. But even Hamlet, throughout his agon, cries implicity: the truth must not be true, the horrible must not be horrible. It is the resistance to a nightmare that makes it a nightmare, however; the fear of the monster is the monster's import. Life is tragic when it feels so. Thus the monster is slain, the nightmare fades, when the resistance is completely monstrous. Then the conscious and unconscious sense of reality become one.

The hero's job is both to resist mortality, glorifying our aspirations, and to embrace it, glorifying our fortitude. Moving in both directions, he becomes more and more, we can say, the victim of his humanity, and his "passion" in the ordinary sense becomes more and more clearly a Passion, the passive endurance of essential mortal pain.

To be embarrassed by the inaction or vacillation of a Hamlet, Antony or Richard II is to feel the point while missing its meaning, to partake of the hero's own pain without yet endorsing it as the play will do. By interrupting the decisive, constructive action in which he has prided himself, the hero is able finally to

48

begin his real experience, to take in what he is, to receive the imprint of his mortality upon his consciousness. To submit, in other words, to his destiny.

In the hybristic condition, the dynamics of mortality must be sensed as other and hostile forces. The resistance itself projects a vision in which life and the gods (its masters) are tyrannical, unfair, grotesque. Here one has the hybristic illusion of the free will to fight an opponent. But through the expenditure of hybris, dualism itself dissolves into mystery. We are tragically bereft of such mental protection: there is no other. The Women of Trachis, Sophocles' play of Heracles, concludes with this dismissal of the chorus:

> You have seen strange things,
> The awful hand of death, new shapes of woe,
> Uncounted sufferings;
> And all that you have seen
> Is God.[14]

It is not that the Greeks externalized the life forces in myth, but that myth demonstrates the externalization of experience through hybris and its potential restoration in tragedy. Tragedy, in other words, actuates myth by dissolving it within the self.

The tragic revelation is, therefore, the experience of the mortal self, organic, unitary and subjectively complete, quite literally identified with destiny and the gods' truth as the myth comes home. In his revelation, tragic man discovers finally that

49

there is will other than free will--the will to be what one must, what, in fact, one already is. He realizes his "necessity" not merely as its victim or as a punished sinner, but as the master of what Joseph Campbell calls his "self-achieved submission."[15] He can like Richard II resolutely pledge himself "sworn brother . . . to grim Necessity," for as Frank Kermode writes perfectly in the New Arden Tempest, "The gods chalk out a tragicomic way, but enforce only disaster. The rest is voluntary."[16] In such enactment of his will, tragic man, alone, assumes all the richness and potency of mortal experience that is his to know.

6. The Sense of Self

As the epigraph to Chapter 2 suggests, popular and journalistic use of the word "tragedy"--naive as it may seem to the critic--sometimes responds to a sense of urgent immediacy, a sense that "tragedy" is emphatically real and personal, as well as irremediable. Because tragedy defines suffering as experience, central to its revelation is the consciousness of selfhood and its implications. In other words, the tragic shock depends on the realization that, unlike merely physical phenomena, what is happening has meaning precisely because it is happening to a self. Now, to be a self in a world of others can be a source of comic liberation and personal power. In the tragic perspective, however, it is this factor, selfhood, that seems to isolate one irretrievably, out of all continuity for all time, from any conceivable context-- physical, social, or cosmic.

" 'People!' " protests a character of Saul Bellow's, " 'But I am not other people. You should realize that. I am--' and she was voice-stopped, she was so angry. 'This is happening to me!' " . . . No understanding can reach the center of this alarm. What is

51

humiliating is that I am humiliated; what is lacerating is that I am torn and mutilated by feeling; what is nauseating is that I am sick; what is terrifying is that I am trapped, for me there is no escape. What has always been obvious is now far more dazzling than obvious. The cliché is alive, and I am humiliated to be caught by a cliché. I am absolutely dependent on an other reality that cannot possibly help for the very reason that it is other. . . . My death is tragic, yours is melodramatic: that is, my experience, the behavior I observe in you. Or, conversely, tragedy is the vicarious experience of my death.

The difference between an event and my consciousness of it cannot be described adequately. It must be made to happen to me. It must, that is, be dramatized, and it must be dramatized not merely as though life were just behavior--the facile method of melodrama.

> The whole content is lost if I think myself safe, or if I look upon the tragic as something alien to myself, or as something that might have involved me but that I have now escaped for good. I would then be looking at the world from the safety of a harbor, as if I were no longer risking body and soul on its troubled seas in search of my destiny.[17]

If high tragedy must be poetic drama it is towards this end: the stylization of reality on an intimately subjective basis, making the dramatic experience the experience of self. The dynamic processes of drama and the suggestive impact of highly charged language project the fiction out of one's own feelings.

We resent being told of tragedy on the highway or in so-and-so's early life, because tragedy cannot be reported. This is the real fallacy of journalistic "tragedy." Though an event may be tragic to the participants, the account of it is tragic only if is presented so that it can be re-presented, so that it can be experienced. It will be experienced as an account, symbolically.

Because poetry is not just words and drama is not just motion, it is inevitable that valid criticism be subjective--not in the sense of idiosyncrasy or relativism, but in an ability to reflect and interpret the literary experience rather than merely the literary work. This principle applies generally but is especially telling in the criticism of tragedy. Thus Aristotle's subjective insight into catharsis remains more suggestive and compelling than his objective descriptions of recognition scenes and the interrelationships of beginnings, middles, and ends.[18] For tragedy depends on the shock, the epiphany: life is what is happening to me.

Through the play-audience relationship of Aristotle's "pity and fear," Sidney's "admiration and commiseration," Shakespeare's "woe and wonder" or (to move a half-step further from object to subject) grief and horror, the play conveys feeling from a fictional center of self to a real self. One is not merely empathic, a relatively sentimental concept in its usual use (How sensitive and caring I am); one experiences feeling as one's own. Ordinary morality and legalism may be explored in the play but they will be explored that they may be exploded, for they are relevant only to

53

behavior. In the moment of shock, when dealing with the phenomenon of another's experience, we find ourselves disarmed of judgment or any recourse to action. Tout comprendre c'est tout pardonner: the tragic dimension of this insight is demonstrated in Mann's Death in Venice. The only appropriate response to another's experience is our own, and that is perhaps the ultimate vulnerability.

The tragic voice functions as a "center of self" within an environment that is stylized to convey otherness. The stylization of externality is one reason why minor characters are minor, often flat and conventionalized, even in Shakespeare. They are the entourage of King Self, who is realized under the conflicting but equally dynamic aspects of potentiality and consciousness. The entourage tend to have behavior rather than experience, contingency rather than potentiality. They are the terms of the environment. Although an absolute sense of self is essential, it can be misleading, therefore, to concentrate on the tragic "hero" as a discrete being; he must also be studied ecologically, for he and his field define each other. He is tragic man because he is imbedded in a tragic world, and both self and world are tragic only in relation to each other, in impact. A Hamlet is tragic because he must live in an Elsinore, and he must. On one level of truth, an Elsinore is tragic--desperate with endless desire--because it must crush the Hamlet that gives it life and light.

A sense of self implies a consciousness of many factors that the self relates to and depends upon. It implies and may explicitly

54

lead to a consciousness of the physical environment and natural forces, of social conditioning, of the phenomenon of dependency itself and its limitations upon the will, of the phenomena of causality and consequence, of recurrent patterns and ironical discrepancies. The consciousness of self is importantly a consciousness of time and of change, the factor that gives time its meaning. The tragic self is caught between the impact of the past and the imminence of the future--"time's winged chariot hurrying near" and "deserts of vast eternity"--especially the future that is no future, the prospect of annihilation, or the impossible future, of a consciousness that one is dead.

Many works, in drama and in other forms, deal with "tragic material" or "tragic plots" yet skirt the actual tragic sense because the immediacy of self-awareness is not part of their dominant effect. In García Lorca's Blood Wedding, such tragic themes are propounded emphatically, but a lyrical consciousness subsumes the sense of self into broad symbolic forces that sweep through the lives of mere characters and overflow in language.

Paintings and sculptures are often profoundly pathetic, expressing radical emotions with vast sympathy, but without a consciousness of self in time they too are not likely to be fully tragic. A work of visual art, furthermore, tends to become more fully itself, an independent other, than a verbal work does. This happens to a degree in any theatrical production, but there remains in the theater a sense that a play's existence is only temporary, in passing, and that its production is only provisional, a

55

version of a play as seen one evening.

Perhaps a film is never fully tragic. We may become more intensely caught up in a movie than in any other kind of work, but we are at the same time the observer of an objective visual reality, which tends to dominate and absorb the language, so that a Shakespeare film is inevitably a struggle between conventions. The film is realized as a work with a degree of finality that sets it apart, self-contained in its own field of space and time, focussing us on images that are completely enmeshed in it. Beyond the throne room at Elsinore is a corridor leading to another chamber and to stairs, etc., and the Olivier/Hamlet who is talking to himself in that room will not leave the theater when the show is over. Thus we go out to the film more than we can take it to ourselves, and are in the end deserted when the lights go on.

Most basically, self implies other. In tragedy the two dimensions are locked together in a death grip. Broadly the whole environment is other, but as drama, of course, a play focusses on the self's relation to other persons. Self is defined by the realization of otherness and other is defined as a perception of self: alteriority and ipseousness, to coin comic grotesques. Because the whole play corresponds to the experience of an individual, there cannot be a one-to-one correspondence between a character and a human being. Like personal images in dreams, the characters--hero or entourage--tend to lack continuous identity (and as in dreams the distinctions tend to be true). The stylized drama of the Greeks and the Elizabethans does not make the deliberate effort to conceal this subjective basis of experience with an encompassing illusion of realism. Through a medium that is ritualistic or lyrical, a reality is evoked that is accurately intimate.

It may be that there are three basic models for the structure of selfhood; we can name them, loosely, for Aristotle, Hegel and Jung, expecting them to overlap. The Aristotelian model presents the self alone and unitary in a world of other. Oedipus Tyrannus and Shakespeare's major tragedies work this way. The self is opposed to a flat world of resistance and pressure even though, as in Lear, the hero may be accompanied in his solitude by sympathizers. The play is constructed to stress the utter aloneness of the self in both its hybris and its suffering, both of which have a magnetic quality, for the aloneness which is the hero's problem is also his strength. "Those who attract most devotion from others," writes Frye, "are those who are best able to suggest in their manner that they have no need of it."[19] This aloneness is achieved even in Antony and Cleopatra where a single center of self is shared between two characters, smothered by the hostile world.

The Hegelian model (prevalent in Greek tragedy?) experiences the simultaneity of two or sometimes three centers of self, each an other to the other but no one qualifying fully as an independent tragic hero. Here we focus on the fact that no point of view has ultimate reality. Life is felt to be tragic because we are vitally dependent on the outside in spite of our uniqueness as selves.

57

In this type of play, we may be more interested in issues than in character. Yet Hegel's self-justifying but hostile orders of good reduce phenomenologically to self and self, with a basic center split tragically between them. Sometimes a character represents this center. There is the Agamemnon truth, extended through Electra, and the Clytemnestra truth, extended through the Furies, with Orestes caught in the middle. There is Phaedra's truth and the truth of Hippolytus, with Theseus split in the middle. The Tamburlaine plays juxtapose the gratification of egocentricity--luxuriant and exultant--with a consciousness of its horrible effect on a world of others who are also selves.

Jean Anouilh's Antigone, which (like the run of French myth plays) may be too reflectively ironic to be fully tragic anyway, opposes the selfhood of Antigone with an equally cogent Creon. However, Sophocles' play is primarily on the Aristotelian model, in spite of Hegel and his own analysis, with its Creon presenting by the end of the play the absolute truth of an otherness to Antigone. When, in this play, she opts for gods and brother, Antigone expresses the way of the personal, of self-fulfillment before all else, while Creon voices the public and pragmatic, the depersonalized values of otherness. Yet one cannot rest content with this explanation, for Creon's hybris is more conspicuous than Antigone's (though less sympathetic) and his subsequent suffering is more clearly a consciousness of self.

The Jungian model presents the self diffused through all or most of the characters, all more or less flat and fragmentary.

58

Here the other is completely internalized, the uniqueness of the self being less emphatic than the horror of being diffused among forces that are mutually destructive and inescapable. The Jungian model can be applied to the "Aristotelian" and "Hegelian" plays as well, since the other is always a projection of the self and someone's otherness is always one's own experience, but it applies more clearly to the tragic experience in Jacobean drama and in modern plays influenced by surrealism. Whether the Duchess of Malfi is a tragic heroine will not tell us whether her play is a tragedy. She is a dimension merely of the tragic self, but so is Bosola, so is the Cardinal, so is Cariola, the maid, who dying releases the shriek of horrible protest we need so badly in our frightened weakness.

No one of the structural theories explains tragedy exclusively, yet they do reduce to a common denominator, their tragic essence, through the discontinuity of selfhood. There are undoubtedly further variations and complications. In Romeo and Juliet we focus selfhood on the young lovers, but the play is fully tragic only if the experience of the others is allowed to touch our consciousness. Their hybristic willfulness both clashes and blends with the earnest devotion of the lovers, and their sense of loss envelops the naive bliss and pathos of the two they lose. And, to cite another variation: although King Lear is surely on the Aristotelian model, it is not crucial whether or not Lear himself achieves a full consciousness of his condition. The play itself achieves consciousness, projecting it on many levels.

7. The Meaning of Death

What is the price of Experience do men buy it for a song
Or wisdom for a dance in the street? No it is bought
    with the price
Of all that a man hath his house his wife his children
Wisdom is sold in the desolate market where none come
        to buy
And in the witherd field where the farmer plows for bread
        in vain

(Blake, The Four Zoas)

On one level, guilt in tragedy is merely the knowledge of mortality. Surely the tragedy of Oedipus does not depend upon a moral feeling for the incest and parricide taboos in themselves. They open up larger issues, compelling a sense of mystery that pierces the nature of nature. As the relationship of generations is reduced to a grotesque parody, the very solidity of coherence is challenged.   Thus the essential limitedness of our situation is experienced pungently. In the proud flowering of his powers the most successful of men can still count on nothing but his vulnerability.   As his knowledge must be limited, so must his powers, and with the best intentions and the keenest genius he

60

swims an ocean of unconsciousness. To know "that we are very dangerous" (Arthur Miller's After the Fall) and to know that we are very vulnerable and to know the interdependence of these facts is to know as experience what it means to say that we are mortal.

Carried a step further, the point seems to turn back on itself: death in tragedy is symbolic of mortal consciousness, including centrally guilt. Traditionally tragedy focusses on the death of a person who lives intensely and frames a show of extravagant vitality around his still corpse. But tragedy is not about death itself, it is about mortal life. It is about the particular problem "That Life lives upon Death" (Blake) while seeming so clearly distinct from it. The literal demise of the hero is the symbol of his conscious commitment to mortal life and the proof of his sincerity. This death is both the effect and the evidence of his mortality as well as his assent to it. The tragic man says he has accepted death, the nadir of reality; we need to see him accept responsibility for his claim by facing its implications. Then we may reward him with our grief.

In other words, the bodily death merely expresses an emotional death. Being merely the vehicle of a symbol, it is arbitrary and need not occur. In fact, the hero "survives his death" in plays as different as Oedipus Tyrannus, Philoctetes and Troilus and Cressida, where his "death" is portrayed in psychological terms only. Characters like Creon of Antigone and Theseus of Hippolytus may be said themselves to "die" in

61

comprehending the significant death of others. At the end of Lear, Kent confirms such a death by saying he will join his master. Whether represented by a literal death or not, the full psychic death of the hero completes typically a process of crucifixion, in which the vigor of his hybris is vigorously mortified. The ego wrenches itself until it shatters the hybristic assumptions on which life seemed in quite an absolute sense to depend. Stripped as "unaccommodated man . . . a poor bare forked animal," the hero finds himself living in the state he knew to be unlivable. He finds himself living, albeit briefly, without the need for protection, in essential humanity.

The mythic motif of "crucifixion" epitomizes the consciousness of mortality through an act of sacrifice. Unlike ritual and comedy, crucifixion and tragedy present sacrifice from the victim's point of view.[20] Doing so, they press home the fact that sacrifice is always implicitly a sacrifice of self, although in ritual and comedy the sense of self is symbolically displaced and externalized upon a surrogate, in order that "rebirth" may be ensured, so to speak, after the kill.

In the "ideal" form of crucifixion (as Christ's) recurrent characteristics all register the extent of human vulnerability: the subject encounters death and endures it, in utter subjectivity. He experiences pain in its extremity, in some form that symbolizes an absolute degree of our capacity for suffering. He undergoes an ordeal of humiliation, usually in the form of a public punishment or a loss of the prerogatives of rank, as the emotional counterpart of physical pain. He submits to his situation, so that it is restrainedly passive; he lets mortality happen to him. In fact, he wills that it happen to him, offering himself for destruction or at least acknowledging that his own desires have led him to it. He is solitary, set apart by an experience that cannot be shared, without refuge from his selfhood. He becomes or remains conscious of what he is going through, so that his relationship to the ordeal becomes a form of knowledge and a form of responsibility. The result of his sacrifice is rebirth, which has the personal level of his own apotheosis and the public level of the salvation he brings others . . . . The logic of "crucifixion" is only implicit in tragedy (or vice versa), but its implicit condition reveals what we may call the symbolic ratio of ordinary psychology. The lecturer on The Wings of the Dove, asked if he thought Milly Theale a Christ figure, replied, "no, but I believe Christ is a Milly Theale figure."[21]

In tragedy, the equivalent of salvation is catharsis. The growth of consciousness which concludes the tragedy by transcending it is usually developed through the hero himself, but what is important is simply that it evolve in the play. It may be dramatized through secondary characters or it may be conveyed tonally. The tonality is supremely important because through it emerges the characters' experience that is also the audience-reader's experience--the tragic sense itself. Within the fiction of the play and beyond it, the hero's death sheds the sense of self around him in his world of otherness: thus the meditative reflections of survivors at the end, struck with an awareness that can lead to no immediate action except funeral rites as they leave the stage unified in solitude, and as we by extension leave the theater. Catharsis exorcises our own otherness, our anxious detachment, that is, from our own feelings.

The hero's "psychic death" makes possible our simulation of dying--or, to put the situation more realistically, the character's fictitious ordeal evokes genuine feelings in us, although they are blended with feelings of esthetic gratification. As I participate really in the imaginary consciousness of Lear or Othello, I die with them. I die as fully as they do themselves, in fact, since their death, like their life, is only an experience of consciousness with no real physical implications. But an essential part of the dramatic experience (to understate) is the fact that I am alive at the end of the play. My dramatic experience does not stop with the death of the hero, even if the play does, which is hardly ever so. I survive perhaps with both some guilt and some complacency, like any survivor. I experience a special guilt and complacency knowing it is all make-believe; but more--since this is an experience I have participated in without real danger--I go through some degree of my own feelings about dying and remain alive with some sense of living solidity.[22]

It is not literal death we or the hero are afraid of--death has no qualities in itself to fear--but it is our feelings about death. The possibility of catharsis lies in the fact that, though death is absolute, our feelings about it only feel absolute. Death, then, symbolizes our surrender to unconscious feelings. On one level the consciousness of mortality is the experiential knowledge of all

64

those factors that separate our capacity for desire from our capacity for fulfillment. On a further level, more directly psychological and less philosophical, the death of the defensive ego promises to leave us exposed to the most deeply fixed feelings that we have about being ourselves, alive.

Our ordinary fear of death may be no more than this vulnerability to our own reality, a fear of no longer being able to protect ourselves from being, or of no longer being able to search out the proof we are not what we suspect we are. Death is the end of recourse. Quite naturally, it is the ultimate revelation of our emotional as well as our physical vulnerability, and it is this conviction of our "mortal weakness" that is most threatening to the tragic selfhood. Through the humiliation, the nausea, the annihilation and the transcendence that constitute the tragic hero's ordeal (and our symbolic participation in it), a clarification of this conviction is mimed.

8. Tragedy and Neurosis

Tragedy probably does reflect the cataclysms of the nursery, as Ernest Jones argued, but the central dimension is not merely the limited Oedipal pattern. If tragedy is neurotic, it still does no good to talk about the hero's neurosis in the spirit of a case study, for, unlike social science, tragic drama speaks in the first person. Its ability to do so is one of the advantages of the dramatic medium. We see around us in the play a neurotic universe, which as his otherness is both a projection of the hero's mind and a definition of his plight. It is not enough to say, as some sympathetic commentators do, that the world is mad and he is not. He is of the world but not in it, trying desperately to keep himself in it but not of it, trying, that is, to be other than neurotic. Yet his resistance is conditioned by the environment he resists. He must be compromised by his society, as he is by his mortality, even though he may see beyond both with his passionate vision.

In this sense, neurosis is the "normal" human predicament, the starting point, and as the most promising psychologists seem to assume, the only way to deal with neurosis is to explore it, to be neurotic in order to be sane, to be neurotic, so to speak, with a vengeance. It is in this spirit that the hero commits himself to the necessary fallacy of his hybris, plunging himself into his passion until, in Blake's phrase, "The road of excess leads to the palace of wisdom."

The hero, naturally, cannot assume that his violence will beget a kind of harmony; he cannot die in order to be reborn, with a return ticket or guarantee. His passion and his death must feel irredeemable to have integrity. They must be dramatized as absolute, and then the flights of angels will sing him aloft one way or another, if only with the song of the dramatist, the play itself.

Overlaid upon the wisdom of sanity is the wisdom of madness, Dionysus poised against Apollo in poignant tension, but it is the wisdom of madness that asks our questions for us and commands our first allegiance. It is Lear's challenge that should trouble the gods, not Edmund's, nor Edgar's. But we would cheat ourselves, too, if we denied completely the clinical or transcendental terms that would see this self-glorifying anguish objectively as a maimed vision. The chorus may speak in fear and the rationalist in chilly detachment. They are humanly wrong but their words, like Polonius', may point, in spite of their own guarded obtuseness, to the genuine perspective that can be acquired and begotten only by plunging ahead into hybris. Before his plunge, the hero starts from where we are. But from the later perspective we may look back through catharsis to see the whole process as a bad dream, as, indeed, a neurotic aberration.

We are not dealing with neurosis as casual or accidental--the result would be melodramatic, with a Hamlet whose problem could have been prevented with proper treatment in time. Nor at the other extreme are we dealing with a psychological determinism, as in O'Neill's plays. This replaces the misinterpretation that Greek plays are supernaturally deterministic with an equally sterile, mechanistic and therefore again melodramatic scheme of life.

Tragedy may be therapeutic, as the truth is (though only tentatively so: how often has anyone been "cured" at the theater?); it is not analytical. It is not concerned with the external forces that make one do what he does but with the state of feeling that drives him and with the impact of his movement. It is not concerned centrally with incidents in the hero's remote or his recent history. The tragic playwright does not look back to the linear causes of his effects (hence the quite adequate vagueness of Iago's motivations) but immediately into their feeling and ahead to their cataclysm.

Although the tragedy of <u>Hamlet</u> is not about Hamlet's childhood, the play as a whole does dramatize pressures which engulf us early in life and the consequent difficulties in being human. But only in a completely implicit way, through the unconscious mind of the play, so to speak, rather than of the fictional hero. We must limit ourselves to psychoanalyzing the tragic process, of which the characters are mere figments.

The neurosis that tragedy presents is the predicament of self in culture, the virtually "universal neurosis." As infants we overflow with experience, living imperiously in absolute Self. In a process that is for all practical purposes necessary, the reality of otherness breaks in upon us with definitive violence as, in parental discipline and the processes of socialization, we are forced to identify ourselves with the outside voices of corrective anger, righteousness and disciplinary education. The voices may speak in innuendoes and jests or in protestations of love and concern; they may communicate unconsciously and in silence. The result must be what we are accustomed to calling alienation (though we see it usually as only a contemporary problem, alienating ourselves all the more), or, in Freudian terms, identification with the introjected authority or, in R.D. Laing's stronger terms, "the devastation of experience."[23]

The overflow of rich feeling, which is love of life and of self, is inverted by blame, anger and deprecation into hatred of life and of self, so that we find ourselves circling a center of pain which we must avoid by all the means that civilization is intended to produce. The psychic death we live in dread of, it would seem, is the feeling that we deserve to die, the burden of generalized guilt--"original sin"--that turns us against ourselves simultaneously on all levels of experience: in anguish with our own feelings (sometimes mythologized as deity), with our bodies (the famous sex disgust of Shakespeare and the Jacobeans), with other people (so that the normal basic relationship in Milton's and in Blake's fallen world is jealousy), and with physical nature.

Though we may concentrate on evidence to the contrary, in this state, at least on the unconscious level, every aspect of life is inevitably problematic. Frustrations proliferate frustrations until we are caught in self-perpetuating self-destruction, which is intensified by the direct effort to escape.

> Alack, when once our grace we have forgot,
> Nothing goes right. We would, and we would not.

We live out of an absolute sense of desire that can never be absolutely gratified. Most centrally we feel we need love but cannot genuinely accept it or give it. Nor can we accept, really, any of the signs of fulfillment that we seem forced to pursue. We are dependent on our judges. The present is merely the past running into the future. We are torn between the hunger for fulfillment and the force of gravity that compels us toward the still untouchable pain within. Essentially, we find ourselves part of a curiously mad world where everyone feels unconsciously that he is the essential outcast while all try to relate to one another as peers. The fabric must hold, or else.

Most laughter is the effect of relief in being let off the hook--whether through the self-elevation of satire, or the detachment from feeling in stylized wit and in farce, or the delight of form fulfilling itself in romance. Laughter recognizes that the disease is not fatal, which is in fact true and a source of revelation: we are not as hopeless as we feel--but it provides a sly escape from feelings to which we are unconsciously committed, and we do not usually trust the escape very far. Tragedy breaks down our defenses against these same feeelings, blocking escape--but it does so by a strategy which leaves as bait one last source of gratification. Through the elegance of form we are allowed the luxury of thinking that we are talking about someone else. . . . Still, if we do admit the dramatic symbolism, allow it to work on us, we are touched. There is then the relief of being seduced into a significant reality.

In traditional plays the tragic self-hatred is often displaced or disguised, the way it usually is in our personalities, with emphasis perhaps on manifestations of the feelings rather than the feeling itself. Where it is most explicit, in Hamlet, centuries of critics have managed to look elsewhere finding confusion, mystery, philosophy. Sometimes the heart of the feeling is externalized on a villain like Iago, whose drive must lack substantial motivation precisely because there is nothing beyond itself. "The cause" is the state of "malignancy"; the tragedy is that there need be no further cause. When Iago says of Cassio:

> He hath a daily beauty in his life
> That makes me ugly . . .

he reveals more about his nature than he does in his "motive-hunting." We experience him directly as a condition of

71

consciousness. In the image of his characterization, that condition is made to seem self-sufficient, but it is also, fundamentally, the aspect of the emotional self which makes Othello's powerful dignity powerfully vulnerable: a reservoir of self-doubt, guarded fury, and the deep fear of scorn.

Similarly, if incestuous drives are relevant to the character of Webster's Antonio in The Duchess of Malfi, they are symptoms only. They are, perhaps, a submerged truth, not concealed but not quite true. We cannot say that they are there unconsciously; they are only potentially there, although they really are potentially there. To say more is to mistake the stylization of such a play, which accurately focusses on the condition of negativity itself. In modern drama the malignancy is more often expressed within the rounded character of the hero, so that many really tragic modern characters--Hedda Gabler, for instance--evoke distaste immediately from reactive readers.

In the tragic complex of emotion, particular feelings are often sophisticated expressions of the radical pain or else reactions against it, controlled and defined below the surface in "the play's unconscious." Tragedy is a world seen through self-hatred; the effect of that feeling is absolute because it corrupts every aspect of one's being and of the world one experiences. When there is self-pity in real tragedy, as in Richard II, it is felt honestly in connection with self-loathing, against which it can represent a heroic resistance, and when there is bitterness it is felt as a vent for a valid desperation.

Guilt and shame are both attacks upon one's selfhood from the perspective of others' eyes. The moralist's vices and the critic's flaws--jealousy, lust for power, ruthlessness, arrogance--all echo the abyss of one's helplessness. Man is always falling. To be, one must be one's own self and if that is intolerable, hope and desire become infinitely pathetic, intense to the bursting point of hybris. When all of life is denied, there will be left, if nothing else, an utter grief, for beneath the passion that would negate all life there persists the still more radical wish to live. The organism will grow, even to decay.

The self accepts the burden of being an other to a hostile world, destroying itself ingenuously as a scapegoat. There is a well-earned credit due this bitter sacrifice but first credit is due the bewildered resistance, because it is a will to affirm being at any cost. Between the willingness to die and the will to live, the sense of a predicament is inevitable: life is impossible, yet we do live; it is a trap, yet to be we must be free; it seems designed for gods (life unalienated), yet bestowed on men; it sounds, looks and smells beautiful, for we are "the paragon of animals!"--"And yet . . . man delights not me"; living requires vast doing, but where it counts most we seem to be powerless; we need each other, yet so often we find our way only to being alone or bringing hurt.

Thus that profound sense of disjunction or discontinuity, which seems so peculiar at first ("Yet who would have thought the old man to have had so much blood in him?"), which is nausea and

73

death, haunting the plays with the heartache of the tragic subjunctive: "if only . . . ," followed at least implicitly by its tragic "but alas . . ."

> If the assassination
> Could trammel up the consequence, and catch
> With his surcease, success . . .

> Thou art a lady;
> If only to go warm were gorgeous,
> Why nature needs not what thou gorgeous wear'st . . .

> If beauty, wisdom, modesty, can settle
> The heart of Antony, Octavia is
> A blessed lottery to him.

> Oh, God, I could be bounded in a nutshell
> and count myself a king of infinite space
> were it not that I have bad dreams.

The subjunctive is our idealism and our blindness, our self-pity and our capacity to love. It expresses, that is, our yearning for a world of really very simple coherence: if only an action could be complete in itself (Macbeth), if only we wanted what we need (Lear), if only we loved what we profess to admire (Antony and Cleopatra), if only our feelings belonged to us to command (Hamlet) . . .

What is not much to ask is far too much to receive, for the subjunctive yearning expresses also how difficult it is to see the source of the frustration, the ghastly mechanism that proliferates consequences of consequences and compels our own feelings against us. The self-pity that the subjunctive expresses insists on

74

reason (Life must be fair!), but it breaks down the facade of reasonableness in sorrow, softening the feelings to their own vulnerability and to a love for the vulnerability of others. The sense of life's value rises spontaneously from the smoldering fire, and the passion for life, for the primeval wholeness that is our birthright, is offered as the essential protest against all the spectres of death that permeate experience.

9. Tragedy and Culture

These "notes" have assumed that tragedy is understood most richly as a symbolic form expressing an intrinsic factor of human consciousness--rather than as a portrayal of personal events. Tragedy, therefore, expresses something significant about the nature of consciousness while, at the same time, it expresses something about the symbolic processes that constitute culture. Accordingly, some thoughts about culture, symbolism and consciousness may suggest the nature of tragedy more deeply than we have gone so far. Caught in the tension between living and dying, consciousness and the unconscious, the world and the void, the tragic hero is both victim and explorer of the phenomenon of symbolism through which he must know himself and confront his nature.

One of the sturdier obstacles to an understanding of tragedy is the kind of relativism--historical and otherwise--that has been an important aspect of modern culture, carrying as it does the persuasive weight of supposedly objective intellectual sophistication. The point will be, generally, that tragedy is different in every age, if not in every playwright, and must be studied pluralistically as the succession of changing conceptions. The relativist is likely to be thorough in his research and modest in his claims. He is interested only in what can be known clearly. He can see too well the fallacies of other periods to risk any himself. To speak of human nature or a tragic vision, he knows, is merely to generalize the image of one's own arbitrary culture, to promote another ethnocentric fallacy that is doomed to join the future's collection of antiquities.

The arguments for this position easily win a consensus one cannot hope to match by suggesting that a further truth remains to be known subjectively with a different sort of reliability. But as long as one is bound to affirm only what will be readily believed, one can never trust what he really knows. History--on either the cultural or political level--is not simply a study of changes, of different events and notions; it is a study of change-in-identity, of reformulations of experience based on the continual reliving of what must recur, as infants grow to childhood, youth to age, and the aged to death--multitudinously, variously, but obsessively repetitive nonetheless. Shelley writes simply and clearly, "The mass of capabilities remains at every period materially the same; the circumstances which awaken it to action perpetually change"--and one will say, "Yes, that is a Romantic attitude." We feel more confident when we know than when we understand.

From epoch to epoch, man shifts his focus of attention. He

77

becomes aware newly of certain aspects of his vista and loses sight of others, stylizing his own conceptions of himself and, in doing so, restructuring his relationship to himself. His vision goes off first in one direction from the center, then in another. What was peripheral becomes focal; tangents turn into new circles of attention. He finds new applications for his formulas and then cannot see the formulas for the applications. In the process, his experience itself changes pitch or key. He hangs his hat in different rooms of his psychic home. What was unthinkable becomes inevitable, what was embraced is dreaded. His different ideas make him think his experience is different, and he asks different questions about it. Often he confuses his ideas with his experience, and at that point he usually prefers to think about ideas.

One obvious principle of cultural change is that, from step to step, what has been discovered comes to be assumed. What has shocked us comes to seem quite indifferent and then we may even reject it by ignoring it. We relate differently to what is true but it remains true just the same. The shift in consciousness is not the same as a shift in knowledge or in belief. Vocabularies change and languages, but we learn to read them, because we can learn to misunderstand them, to see their assertions all as human possibilities in spite of literal differences.

It is safer and more scientific to consider that meaning is a function of language, that meaning is, in fact, created by what we say and write and put on stage. But this is a limited truth.

Language may direct and temper thought, but it is not only thought that we strive to express. We struggle with extraordinarily inadequate tools and very dim vision to grasp qualities of reality that are literally infinite in complexity because they are not divisible at all. Meaning is the silent echo of words. Inevitably, we communicate through symbols and signs, but we can communicate because symbols, in Coleridge's phrase "partake of the reality that they render intelligible."[24] We must read them by intuitive reference back to reality through their unspoken implication, which we can do because they partake of it. Such symbolic formulations of experience--such myths--differ on a principle, as shadows cast from a figure at different angles all refer to the same solid shape, as one's own changing feelings day by day cohere and reflect each other if only in unconscious shadows. These shape-shifting myths of life refer back to an archetypal form which isolates the rhythm and structure of life itself. The archetype is not merely a skeleton within an image but a radiation, a dynamic force that the image unleashes.

No human force can be as destructive as myth, but the myth that kills is the myth mistaken for theology, ethics, political necessity or economic expedience, the myth that becomes a tool for practical power by being believed in and taken literally. In myth itself--and the literary styles informed by myth, particularly tragedy and romance--the assertion is qualitative, a thrust of structured experience. Negative implications are simply not on the same level as the positive assertion, and the ironist's implications ("Yes, but on the other hand . . . ") are not continuous with it. The form and constitution of the myth limits, therefore, the way it can validly be applied to the world at large.

Since myths are qualitative assertions, also, we should be slow to analyze any literal connections between them. They inevitably complement one another but each in its own terms. Each makes a fresh start, projecting experience to imaginative forms. As we study the changing shape of culture, properly we reduce the projections and think about the radical states that project them. Intuitively, from our own depths, we sense the figure distended in the shadows, although we may never know it in any other way. Our bodies of self-expression are as we are ourselves, variations on a theme. When we see variations only, we reject communication. When we look only for the theme, of course, we lose the texture of particular reality. When we study the tension between the two we grapple with the basic problem of consciousness, each person's need to be his own human self.

To study merely the history of ideas is to give ideas a false autonomy whereas ideas are only one part of one way in which the consciousness of any period manifests itself, for the "consciousness of a period" is always a state of tension between consciousness and unconsciousness. Ideas in themselves do not exist, but myths do because they incorporate the unconscious. When the truth of a myth is grasped, its limitations emerge significantly, therefore, not as a criticism but as an appropriate consequence. What we have then is a history of consciousness which is also a history of unconsciousness. It is the history of man as a creature struggling to formulate experience and to control experience with his formulations, but whose capacity to do both is limited first of all by his flickering awareness of what his experience is and secondly by the nature of the symbolic process that is at work. For the symbol reveals and conceals, as Carlyle says;[25] it reveals by concealing. It grasps experience by distorting it, inverting it, perhaps transcending it but certainly transmuting it.

The symbol or symbolic form--the poem, doctrine, institution or myth--is at once opaque and to varying degrees transparent. There is a tension between communicating and creating, between getting through and blocking attention, between encountering life and substituting for it, between accepting reality and elevating it. Culture, the sum of our symbols, allows us to relate to ourselves only indirectly and only through exaggeration, for all statements are overstatements as all quotations are out of context. The absolutism with which tragedy speaks is a perfect example. As Hesse's Steppenwolf is told, by the mysterious author of the Tractate:

> All interpretation, all psychology, all attempts to make things comprehensible, require the medium of theories, mythologies and lies; and a self-respecting author should not omit, at the close of an exposition, to dissipate these lies so far as may be in his power.[26]

Every statement is a complex of sound and silence.[27] Within the silence live the cry and the laughter that need no language. In a given tragedy it is generally necessary to

81

distinguish archetypal tendencies from the often louder cultural accretions. Thus in <u>Oedipus</u> <u>Tyrannus</u> Oedipus makes the gesture of self-immolation with fully appropriate force--dramatically and mythically--but explains it in the idiom of a shame culture: how can he face his parents in Hades having eyes to behold them? In <u>Oedipus</u> <u>at</u> <u>Colonus</u> the sage faces his transcendence with the bitterness of an injured parent and citizen. The playwright thinking and making is not likely to be completely at one with his mythic inspiration. Perhaps he would not write if he were. The more conscious side of his imagination, at any rate, effects a kind of displacement of the myth, adjusting it to his culture's values.

We have been skirting between two conceptions of myth. First, myth is the wavering half-truth of our attempts to identify ourselves through protean <u>versions</u> <u>of</u> <u>reality</u>, our personalities individually and culturally, the factor of <u>variation</u> <u>on</u> <u>the</u> <u>theme</u>. But also, myth can be understood in an ultimate--or archetypal-- sense. Myth is Truth, the <u>theme</u> upon which variations are played. It is our home in a universe that shares our reality, whose reality we share. Let us say that <u>myths</u> are efforts to approximate or grasp portions of <u>Myth</u>, which we know through such manifestations although it itself is real in a way they are not. Culture consists of myths, but Myth is the principle by which we are related to culture and culture is related to the world.

Myth's archetypal pattern of death and rebirth affirms a coherence of life, of the human place in nature. Myth must deal, however, with its own degeneration, with the breakdown of its

82

own symbolic coherence. The underworld to which the hero descends is the chaos of mythlessness. In other words, tragedy is a dimension or a phase of archetypal Myth. It is the arc of which Myth is the circle. But at the same time we can say that tragedy is Anti-myth, or the myth of Mythlessness. Hybris is a determination to make the arc straight. It is a commitment to the rational over-simplification of life. But Myth is the circularity of the circle, which leads the law of tragic gravity into its corollary law of grace.

* * * * *

The paradox that symbols reveal by concealing is the crucial fact in the study of culture; it might well provide the basis for all education, at least of all criticism. It takes our attention from the apparent reality of symbols as objects in their own right--whether they are observed as masterworks, delusions or data--and focusses on the immediate process of their projection and experience, as the process reconstitutes itself with changing emphases. It makes clear, ultimately, that the nature of culture is the nature of the consciousness that studies it. The real culture is our use of forms, languages and ideas, culture's myths. We cannot avoid the trap: we are caught in our symbols; but the solution of the problem is indicated as the trap is encompassed in consciousness. We sense then that the fundamental and irreduceable reality of the self experiencing its symbols, the subject, is free and innocent, alive in culture but not bound to it.

The problem of culture lies not in any particular symbolic forms or in the fact that we use symbols--but in the nature of our commitment to our symbols, in our willingness to get lost in them--tragically--as in a jungle. Culture has, therefore, an intrinsically tragic dimension, while the direction of consciousness leads toward innocence. It is, in fact, the caught mind's desperation for freedom that creates the utter poignance of tragic emotion, both the strain and the grandeur of its effort.

10. Modern Tragedy

As the stylization of art slackens toward realism, the intensity of the tragic imagery diminishes. Other senses of reality enter into consciousness--irony, ambivalence, the normality of mediocrity, the diffuseness of ordinary experience-- qualifying the complex of tragic emotion out of its sharply definitive form. Yet it would be wrong to assume that tragic import is foreign to these new works or that their tragic import is not essentially the same as it has always been. We may want to distinguish "high" tragedy from, say, tragic drama. However, it is not the tragic that has changed, but its context--or, rather, its relation to context.

Perhaps the most important change in modern plays that are tragedies is that what was traditionally metaphoric becomes literal and relatively direct. The paraphernalia of supposedly external forces--oracles, ghosts and gods--are superseded by unconscious forces that they have always symbolized. What was called the king is shown to be the socially esteemed egoist. Oswald Alving's disease is startling because of its very specificity.

85

It is not that belief has gone in modern times, because tragedy was never really theological and it has always seen belief as hybris. It is not that man has lost his dignity; tragedy, in a way, has always been about the illusion that he ever had any. What is usually gone is the poetic thrust of symbolic concentration, the poetic suggestiveness which expands out of time and place to an infinity of felt presence. General Gabler's pistols and the wild duck cannot gather that force, because they are self-conscious local symbols framed within the plays. In fact, they stand out from their frames and tend to overawe the symbolic force of the plays themselves. High tragedy is "high" because it easily permits the over-statement required for a full, absolute emotional truth. As the symbols are clarified, however, their discontinuity decreased, there is a lessening of power; they become, that is, less symbolic.

If the nature of tragic consciousness does not change, the way of relating to it does change somewhat, both in approach and reaction. At different times the revelation comes in answer to different questions. At some times the revelation is harder to absorb than at others. Each age, as Susanne Langer writes, is characterized by the questions it asks rather than by the answers it finds.[28] It is "who?" (mythically), or "why?" (metaphysically) or "how?" (scientifically), but the answer for the artist at least, always remains life itself. Changes in the imaginative activity that develops a tragic vision effect the total communication taking place. They evoke subtly different responses to the vision, each typifying its ethos, but they do not substantially alter the vision itself. In the history of tragedy, the ancient ritual mode of confronting experience gives way to the rhetorical mode (from Seneca to the neoclassical quasi-tragedy) and to the primarily lyrical (from Marlowe and Shakespeare, against a Christian background, to the romantics). The dominant modern mode would seem to be the analytical, which deals with life by explaining it. We grasp our experience explanatorily.

Characteristic of the modern approach to experience has been a need for the solid continuity of cause-effect relations which leaves us particularly stunned by their breakdown in the most important places, when there is no reason why. Our reliance on objective detachment leaves us all the more helpless before the subjectivity of the tragic content. Through the terms of sociology, psychology, metaphysics and economics, our more realistic plays grasp at experience by delineating relationships between people, between generations, between classes, between the sexes, between society and the individual, so that there develops a special consciousness of theme. We have been taught to expect a play to be about something, not just to be a tragedy or a comedy. However, when such plays are tragic, they are so for the same reason any plays are tragic, because they record an appropriate awe before the spectacle of hybris.

When the analytic tendency dominates the tragic, the result is the "problem play." Though we are told that emotional impact serves to make a serious play entertaining, however, "theme" is often a moral sugar-coating for the emotional heart of the play.

87

Many modern plays based on a depth psychology or a committed sociology lapse into deterministic melodrama, like so much of O'Neill, or into a kind of satire-of-the-pathetic, like Death of a Salesman, but the dramatization of a tangible unconscious, which may have been Ibsen's greatest contribution, does not preclude real tragedy. It requires, as in Strindberg even more than in Ibsen, a less dignified look into the abyss, but it does not diminish the profundity of the abyss or the violent discontinuity between it and the texture of our everyday lives, the discontinuity which provokes the basic tragic recoil.

In Hedda Gabler and The Wild Duck, in The Father and Miss Julie we see central characters who could easily be dismissed as case studies (and often are by unsympathetic readers) were it not that their "cases" are eccentric only in their transparent clarity and their concentration. (One can say the same about most real-life "cases" as well.) They thrive on all sorts of objectionable drives--selfishness, cold hatred, jealousy, the protection of one's weakness, the projections of paranoia, the will to self-dramatization. They are obsessive and petty and infantile. We feel particularly uneasy about calling them heroes. But what is disturbing about them is their own disturbance. Since we are obliged to know these characters internally as consciousness and experience, we come to know them in terms of the predicament they are caught in. We come to sense of them, as we do of any tragic characters, the heroically futile struggle against their predicament. The Wild Duck is an exception in this respect, since both Gregers Werle and Hjalmar Ekdal are portrayed satirically.

88

However, a sense of tragedy in the play still develops around Gregers as center of self, absorbing into his "heroic" ambiance the girl, Hedwig, and Hjalmar her father, who are in themselves only pathetic in very different ways.

In both the male and female characters of these plays by Ibsen and Strindberg, we see a complementary reaction against the inevitable imposition of roles, the woman's supposed docility yielding to viciousness, the man's supposed competence revealing an absolute weakness that is a fear of weakness. Beneath all the roles is an avalanche of semi-conscious self-disgust that must destroy in and out. It is the predicament of a commitment to hostile forces, a dependency on the values and needs of others, which will kill because they too, those social drives, are reflexes of internal poisoning. Most people, in the plays and in the audiences, will object to the feelings and the predicament. The tragic dramatist reveals the nauseous anguish of the consciousness caught within them. He does so more metaphorically in an era of symbolic density, when myths and ceremonies abound; in modern drama he does so more naturalistically.

From Chekhov to the absurdists, another change in stylization is apparent. A tonality contained within Shakespeare's tragic vision becomes itself the encompassing structure of feeling: a tension between tragedy and comedy which is not the integrating overview of romance but a consciousness of static ambivalence. Although in any play, or in different productions, emphasis can lead in either direction, there is a pivotal feeling of the tragedy of comedy and the comedy of tragedy, of the sense in which life is all the more painful because of its triviality and all the more ludicrous because of its urgent self-seriousness. The grotesque absurdity that belongs to the heart of all tragedy becomes the total perspective. It itself is affirmed with the absoluteness of accurate overstatement so that further context would be distortion. The result is so highly stylized that in the plays of Beckett, Ionesco and Pinter we are back to a genuinely poetic drama. It lacks the tonal range of high tragedy, especially the softness of its sorrow (the most basic difference between King Lear and Endgame), but it is the closest thing we have to it. In order to be metaphoric, it must be self-conscious, and the self-consciousness itself becomes tragic, the playwright engaging us with him in a death struggle against his form.

Ionesco's Exit the King (Le roi se meurt) is an absurdist paradigm of tragic disintegration in which "the king" is at once every man about to face his insubstantiality and the entire race about to expire. It succeeds in carrying the pathetic "common man" closer to tragedy than a realistic technique is likely to do because it conveys by caricature the absolute grotesqueness of his situation. In The Chairs, similarly, the forms of logic, language, narration and historical reality are parodied comically, but the grotesqueness of the comedy becomes nightmarish as the structure of personality crumbles into savage drives for attention. The infantile hunger for mama, the fantasies of sexual desirability, the lust for power and for prestige, the blind desire to communicate when there is nothing to say and no language to say it in, and, most basically, the compulsion to nurse outlandish illusions--all struggle against the equally desperate social tie between the old man and his age-old marriage partner. The effect is deeply pathetic as well as satiric; however, there can be no sense of a superior consciousness indulging in sympathy or in satire, for the Old Man and Old Woman are not simply a senile pair of individuals but a highly stylized representation of our usual nature. At the end they leap to non-apotheosis while the hired orator declaims wretched syllables on their behalf, but one has the sense that it is all an account of what is going on at every moment, life perpetuating itself in utter tragic impossibility.

What a coherent culture provides the writer of traditional tragedy is not merely a belief in deity or arbitrary moral standards--these are symbols or symptoms of the condition--but the provisional authentication of his own experience, the starting assumption of its validity in the terms through which he readily perceives it. Without this packaged authentication, he must twist against his own distrust of himself, issuing his experience through the double obstacle of plays about plays, expressing his feelings through a distrust of feeling. It is the trick of the double negative: he is not not having experience. His guilt for using forms, for proffering his experience, is exorcised by the creation of a form that is officially formless. The process is a kind of ritual sacrifice, a self-affirmation through self-immolation.

If we consider the possibility that culture as we generally know it is a defense against unconscious pain--concealing more than revealing--it follows that cultural movements take place as

91

we come to see through our own defenses and no longer feel protected by them. Two things can happen: we grasp around for new defenses, reactions against the exposed ones, and we come closer, with resignation and desperation, to the radical feelings within. The defensive structure was a reasonable simulation of real life, providing some range of possibilities in spite of its reactiveness. We could sing, if not too happily, we could play, though excelling at tragedies, and we could accomplish work, though under the spell of anxiety. In losing defensive power we sink into despondency. Yet the sinking, the decadence, confirms the more substantial prime level of hurt energy, which can now command our attention in its own right. Down on the curve is up.

Curiously, it has sometimes seemed that modern man must be unable to create tragedy precisely because his culture has been itself more tragic, more thoroughly committed to the probabilities of collapse and futility than the possibilities of integration and growth. Consequently, our plays lack the preliminary grandeur and the concluding restitution we associate with high tragedy. That is, they lack the process of revelation and recoil and the impetus with which hybris thrusts ahead. Our tragedies often lack a clearly focussed catharsis, but perhaps that is because the pain is so immediate and pervasive. In lesser playwrights it may be too close to be close enough, so it is kept at a distance with ostentation and sentimentality--but this has always been so.

However, though we get nothing sometimes but the bottom of the circle, we are still on the same circle and it is the same bottom. And if this presentation is less spectacular and stirring, it has another kind of dramatic value, which reveals another kind of truth. The symbols of a culture, it shows, trap us in their spell, then leave us helpless before the very depths they eloquently speak of. Perhaps tragedy has always been about the destruction of one's symbol system, one's means of interpreting the world.[29] It has, in fact, suggested that the only meaningful story is the tale told by an idiot signifying nothing, but a meaningful story it thereby still has been. Now, as in The Chairs, both the silence and the babble may seem to drown out the voices that would be eloquent about them. But also, we may wonder whether there is not now more possibility, in a more immediate way, of accepting what has always been true and has generally been known. The symbol conceals by revealing. Now, when we have felt most dubious, anxious and dispersed, perhaps we can better attain a liberating perspective on culture and all its cults, so that symbols can be free in consciousness, working and playing for us with something essential of innocence.

BLAKE'S MYTH OF INNOCENCE

An Approach to Symbolism

"How is it we have walkd thro fires

& yet are not consumd"

The Four Zoas

1. The Singer and the Song

As someone must have said: a poem means what it does; it should not be but do. Kenneth Burke's approach, as it is presented in The Philosophy of Literary Form, "assumes that the poem is designed to 'do something' for the poet and his readers, and that we can make the most relevant observations about its design by considering the poem as the embodiment of this act."[1] Like any symbolic form, a poem exists only in the dynamics of perception, when an adequate sense of its potentiality is realized. It communicates through its structure, to be sure, as a created thing, but what should matter to us most is not the contours of the structure in themselves, but the condition of consciousness that the structure, by design, produces. The symbol projects its own unique experience and it is for that that we cherish it. We submit to the symbol, receiving its stimuli, understanding it perceptually as it acts upon us. We are not always aware of what we are experiencing, and our conscious efforts to interpret often obscure and distort what is really happening. Individual readings are bound to vary, yet one can come to recognize a substantial aspect of the experience which is the heart of the symbol. The symbol is an

97

organism preserving its experience. It is also a device designed to foster its meaning, which it does by inducing in us its own special experience. The meaning is what the poem makes happen.

Probably no poet illustrates this general process more clearly than Blake. Obviously Blake's Songs of Innocence conveys a conception of what innocence is, and as readers we wish to grasp the essence of it. However, the songs define innocence through the song process; it is not simply a subject of the verses. In many ways, simply but richly, they render innocent music, and innocence is what they do. Some of the ablest Blake critics interpret the more elusive of these lyrics ironically; but irony is the opposite of innocence, it is the mode of experience. These are not only songs of innocence, they are innocent songs, and they require innocent singing, for it is not enough that they be heard, they must be joined, and as we join them, we become what we hear. Irony is exorcised, we become innocent. There is nothing more important for the songs to communicate.

As we sing, we become naturally the voice of the song each in ourselves. In the "Introduction" I am

> Piping down the valley wild
> Piping songs of pleasant glee[2]

and the wildness of the valley becomes a pleasantly gleeful wildness, which makes an effortless reach from valley to cloud, from singer to child.

Frontispiece to
Innocence
            British Museum

On a cloud I saw a child.
And he laughing said to me.

He did not demand or request, exhort, instruct or intimate, but merely <u>said</u>. It seems too strong to say even that he told me to do it.

And he laughing said to me.

Pipe a song about a Lamb

He said it <u>and</u>, I responded <u>so</u>:

So I piped with merry chear,

it all taking place paratactically, that is to say innocently, innocent of any reaction on my part and of any particular kind of cause-and-effect. It just happened, spontaneously, naturally.

So I piped with merry chear,
Piper pipe that song again--
So I piped, he wept to hear.

My piping with merry chear produced its inevitable result, not its effect but its unfolding. Next a saying occurred that I repeat my song. And again I naturally piped, <u>comma</u>, he wept to hear, <u>without pause</u>, <u>explanation or fullstop</u>. My merry "chear" became his weeping to hear, on the flow of my melody. And along the influence of the child-voice the piping became singing became writing down

In a book that all may read--

illuminated, of course, with a picture of the process taking place, all senses flowing together.

So he vanish'd from my sight.

I was singing him and writing him. He vanished from my sight to become my song. (No, that sounds too deliberate--yet it is not untrue.)

And I pluck'd a hollow reed.

And I made a rural pen,
And I stain'd the water clear,
And I wrote my happy songs

And I did it and I did. How could it have been otherwise? and what is there to explain? One step leads to another, but not in causation, or merely in sequence. It all just takes place.

Every child may joy to hear

Is that the purpose or the result? It is the nature of the song itself. It is innocence, made to happen through a story-song-picture process as the realization of a desire and the clarification of an impulse.

Through the song, the <u>wild</u> takes in <u>the</u> <u>child</u>, <u>chear</u> leads to <u>hear</u>. That all may read, I pluck'd a reed. Daringly, I stained the water clear, its stained clarity becoming the joy of child-hearing, every-child-hearing. The ironist may hear a sinister echo in the hollow reed and a nervous self-consciousness in the creation of a rural rather than an urban pen and, certainly, a moral ambiguity in the staining of the water. But the singing process gathers in the quality of the images and sloughs off their "implications" as individual clusters of words. The images must lead to happy song and they can do so only through happy song. We are aware only that the hollowness of the reed makes it fragile and airy. Through it will flow words, not merely ink, just as music flows through the reeds of the pipe. The rural pen is what will emerge from a reed. The stain leads us to the church window perhaps but not to the confessional. The images are themselves innocent.

The only natural way to read Blake, or any other poet, is to let the meaning emerge from the feeling of the poetry. Tone, the quality of the voice, has priority over any external information, any similarities found in other poems, any systematic implications of the author's philosophy or mythology. Such factors may confirm or clarify what we sense in the poems. They can be invaluable to focus what we half-sense or to bring out features that fit into the direct experience. But the direct experience comes first (and what we know of human nature comes second). Once we sense the organic form to this degree, we can accomodate whatever else will be appropriate to it.

2. The Myth of the Symbol

A <u>symbol</u> <u>is</u> <u>an</u> <u>expression</u> <u>of</u> <u>reality</u> <u>that</u> <u>takes</u> <u>on</u> <u>a</u> <u>reality</u> <u>of</u> <u>its</u> <u>own.</u> The poem, that is, is a real poem, presenting a unique experience, but one that is projected, or refined, from the context of immediacy. Im-mediately, we cry, exult, hunger for reasons of our own. The poem causes us to rehearse our own intimate feelings while we focus upon its fiction, its imagery. In the process of expressing immediate reality, a symbol also expresses the experience of itself. The experience of the symbol can be viewed as the immediate reality of an <u>esthetic</u> experience, so that one can write a poem about reading Chapman's Homer and someone else a poem about reading Keats' poem about reading Chapman's Homer.[3]

The symbol is a combination of two tendencies, each an effort to fulfill one of the realities. It releases a <u>centrifugal</u> tendency which is allegory, a consciousness of relevance to the immediate and open-ended human context. Whenever we generalize about a fiction--read universal meaning in it--we understand the symbol allegorically. Thus every hero is

Everyman, the self, every rose the beauty of love. However, this allegorical tendency has the potentiality of being conceptualized in many ways unless it is deliberately restricted by formal allegorical signs, like Good Works, Youth or the Kingdom of Heaven. The symbol itself can be described as the concrete condition of such potentialities.

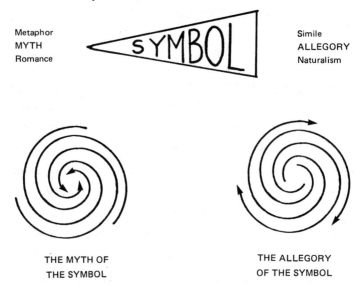

Metaphor
MYTH
Romance

Simile
ALLEGORY
Naturalism

THE MYTH OF
THE SYMBOL

THE ALLEGORY
OF THE SYMBOL

The symbol focusses, with its main force, a centripetal tendency toward metaphor and myth. If symbol is an expression of reality that takes on a reality of its own, the myth--in this primarily literary sense--is that tendency of a symbol to take on its own reality, to become itself; and it is also the reality which the symbol consequently does take on. Every work of fiction, every lyric, and every painting as well, achieves its own concrete world that must be understood as substance, qualitatively. Each of these worlds is discontinuous from every other, yet each must

104

be understood in the continuity of projection. From one symbol to another, the drive in each direction--toward myth and toward allegory--is more or less strong. One important way of understanding any symbolic utterance, therefore, is to gauge its balance of tension in this respect.[4] Another way, related to this, is to grasp its ontological status, the kind of reality that it achieves in relation to immediacy.

Symbol as a thing is illusion, and though it is one of the functions of art to create just that illusion, the symbol must be understood otherwise, behind its own back, not as a thing in itself but as a process. The process of projection is the continuity between the living mind and its images, between artist and beholder, between immediate experience and esthetic experience. We need to study not symbols especially but symbolism, and this is implicitly a study of the mind, a study of our active existence in the history of consciousness. We see ourselves in the mirror but we can see ourselves more significantly in the drives that lead us to the mirror.

The myth of the symbol exerts its centrifugal force by a tendency to generalize itself, radiating significance. It suggests implications but these do not have the same kind of reality as the symbol has qualitatively. They have the reality of suggestions rather than of facts. The most direct way of reading symbols, however, and the richest, is to emphasize the myth in itself as the heart of the symbol, as its potentiality to have significance. The symbol has been compared to a mathematical formula which can

105

be applied to any number of termini while still retaining its own identity.[5] It remains in itself a pattern of relationships, no matter how it is applied.

In poetic significance, the symbolic form is perceived qualitatively. What are usually called its meanings by various commentators are just various potential termini. They are not wrong, unless they are outrageous, yet none of them can be the meaning of the symbol. They are more or less tangential, often going off on their own. They may always be relevant, but they are sometimes of so little relevance that they hardly exist. The symbol's real meaning is its potentiality of application. We can extend the point, however, by saying that the different levels of reality to which the symbol applies are also symbolic of one another; the central esthetic form that suggests them all suggests as well that they are all extensions of each other into different practical categories of reality. Things equal to the same thing are equal to each other.

In Moby Dick Ahab, Starbuck and Stub study the doubloon posted on the mast and read it allegorically, each interpreting it with his civilized intelligence according to his personal bent. Then less sophisticated members of the crew read it in different sorts of literal ways. Finally the mad boy Pip sees the process itself and makes a symbolic reading: "I look, you look, he looks; we look, ye look, they look." With irrational directness, he performs the function of the novelist himself and proceeds to mythologize the experience in fantastic terms that encompass the entire situation and expand beyond it from within.

The conception of the mythic dimension of every symbol emphasizes that in every symbol an ontologically discrete reality is projected. The symbol is not just a rhetorical tool, a means toward an end; it has body and weight. It is opaque and stops the vision--or, rather, it is translucent, like stained glass, and infuses the vision with significance. There is created a world in which I do become a piper and a child and a lamb with no breach of my own identity (because I am a piper and a child and a lamb). There is created, in The Songs of Experience, an order of nature in which a rose can be sick (not blasted or blighted), in which a worm can be invisible and can fly in the night with the power of a dark secret love. There is created the tyger, rather than a tiger. We do not confuse these species with the garden variety of the flower or the jungle variety of the beast, nor do we extend the species beyond the specimen. Probably the kinds are ontologically distinct from one another as well as from their cousins in nature, yet the concrete specimens of the imagination are all equally valid within their appropriate ontology. Their truth is not given as it were; we are required, quite urgently, to confront the truth that it is so, the poem's mythic truth. Imagination is the way in which we realize the mythic reality, and care about it. Instead of saying that these myths are created, in fact, we should say that truths are perceived in the process of mythic representation. Perhaps we should say that the myths are "grown."

Myth is creative; however, it is not merely esthetic. Blake

emphasizes that it ("vision") is esthetic.

> A Poet a Painter a Musician an Architect: the Man
> Or Woman who is not one of these is not a Christian
> (<u>Laocoon</u>)

But it is the creativity of art that makes it an essential life-force.

> The unproductive Man is not a Christian much less the
> Destroyer   (<u>Laocoon</u>)

And it is the creation of <u>forms</u> (that is, of myths) which confirms art's role in perceiving the <u>manifestation</u> of reality.

> In a work of Art it is not fine tints that are required
> but Fine
> Forms, fine Tints without, are loathsom
> (<u>Public Address</u>)[6]

For the reality created in art is blended with the reality that it perceives.

> Vision or Imagination is a Representation of what Eternally
> Exists. Really & Unchangeably.
> (<u>A Vision of the Last Judgment</u>)[7]

Mythic reality is constituted by an imaginative exercise, yet it is merely <u>identified</u>; the constitution of myth is an identification of reality. A particular myth determines a particular kind of reality within a range of possibilities.

At the same time that we must encounter the myth substantially, we must grasp the sense in which it is so. The word-image structure is itself a terminus in the process of projection-- like the movie screen, which cuts off the beam of patterned light in order to hold the beam's patterns and reveal its image. Although the metaphor may not work at this level in terms of the movie projector, the point is essential in terms of the imagination. For the poem's reality does not reside in images themselves. When we say that the "world" of the symbol is mythically real, we mean that its being depends wholly upon its relationship with the projecting mind.

Everything depends upon what the verb to be means, explicit or understood:

> 1. The Last Judgment when all those are Cast away who trouble Religion with Questions concerning Good & Evil or Eating of the Tree of those Knowledges or Reasonings which hinder the Vision of God turning all into a Consuming fire When Imaginative Art & Science & all Intellectual Gifts all the Gifts of the Holy Ghost are lookd upon as of no use & only Contention remains to Man then the Last Judgment begins & its Vision is seen by the Imaginative Eye of Every one according to the situation he holds
> (A Vision of the Last Judgment)[8]

> 2. The Greeks represent Chronos or Time as a very Aged Man this is Fable but the Real Vision of Time is in Eternal Youth I have however somewhat accomo-dated my Figure of Time to the Common opinion as I myself am also infected with it & my Visions also infected & I see time Aged alas too much so
>   Allegories are things that Relate to Moral Virtues Moral Virtues do not Exist they are Allegories &

dissimulations But Time & Space are Real Beings a
Male & a Female Time is a Man Space is a Woman &
her Masculine Portion is Death
(A <u>Vision</u> <u>of</u> <u>the</u> <u>Last</u> <u>Judgment</u>)[9]

3.   To my Friend Butts I write
My first Vision of Light
On the yellow sands sitting
The Sun was Emitting
His Glorious beams
From Heavens high Streams
Over Sea over Land
My eyes did Expand
Into regions of air
Away from all Care
Into regions of fire
Remote from Desire
The Light of the Morning
Heavens Mountains adorning
In particles bright
The jewels of Light
Distinct shone & clear--
Amazd & in fear
I each particle gazed,
Astonished Amazed
For each was a Man
Human formd. Swift I ran
For they beckond to me
Remote by the Sea
Saying. Each grain of Sand
Every Stone on the Land
Each rock & each hill
Each fountain & rill
Each herb & each tree
Mountain hill Earth & Sea
Cloud Meteor & Star
Are Men seen Afar.
(Letter to Butts, 2 Oct., 1800)

4.   Prisons are built with stones of Law, Brothels with
bricks of Religion.
The pride of the peacock is the glory of God.

> The lust of the goat is the bounty of God.
> The wrath of the lion is the wisdom of God.
> The nakedness of woman is the work of God.
> Excess of sorrow laughs. Excess of joy weeps.
> The roaring of lions, the howling of wolves, the
> raging of the stormy sea, and the destructive
> sword, are portions of eternity too great for
> the eye of man.
> (The Marriage of Heaven and Hell, plate 8)

The meaning of _is_ is never the same but gets continually redefined. The drama of each scene, the structure of each tableau, creates its own criterion by which its truth is known. Ontology is controlled by the account the myth makes of itself. But we never translate such mythic utterances with condescension: the poet says it is so because he is a poet whereas we understand it is not really so. The poet is not simply trying to shock us by overstating, by pretending his fiction is real. As mythmaker he affirms a genuine need, on behalf of accuracy, to say _it is so_, because, in the sense we must discover through the substance of the myth and which we cannot translate at all, it _is_ so.

The mythic language requires that we comprehend reality concretely by working into the particular myth's substance. It is one of the difficulties (or mysteries) of the process, in fact, that an elucidation of the mythic ontology tends to dispel the kind of myth that lives upon direct and simple conviction. For a mental framework like Blake's, differentiation can be destructive of meaning. Theology and esthetics ultimately remain undistinguishable, vision being the all--the seeing and the seen and even the seer himself.

111

3. Towards "True" Myth

The conception of myth is multifarious, having various meanings which overlap. In the study of literature one can treat as myth:

1. specific images or conceptions within a poem, whether these are

a) symbols from religious mythmaking, like Zeus and Brahma, or simulations of them, like Blake's "giant forms"

b) vivid characters, places, incidents, etc., that project generalized (allegorical) significance: the hero as everyman, the environment as microcosm, the plot as the longest journey

c) metaphors and similes that transmute reality into conceptions of reality, blending disparate kinds of being into a new order: the sick rose but also the rose which is not merely a red but a red, red rose

2. The work itself, the fiction of the narrative, the play or poem as a vision

3. the genre, such as tragedy, epic or romance, as visions of

life, ways of seeing, stylized aspects of experience

4. nonliterary cultural forms that infuse the work--religious, social and moral myths, etc.: the Christianity reinvented in a play of Shakespeare's but also the feudalism, the code of honor, the cosmology, the conventionalization of love

We have been using "myth" on one level, to mean qualitative assertion or any version of reality. On a more specialized level (though a more familiar one)--what can be called, for the sake of distinction, "true myth"--the term suggests a penetration to the essential nature of human experience, made by conspicuously violating features of observable reality (time and space, cause--effect, identity, growth and decay, etc.). It suggests irreduceable contours of life (archetypal patterns) in a way that evokes a sense of wonder toward their being in themselves, a sense of the "miracle" that what is _is_.

"A Cradle Song," in Songs of Innocence, is obviously a lullaby:

> Sweet dreams form a shade,
> O'er my lovely infants head.

but the effect of this lyric is not merely to pacify a baby. It produces peace by integrating the mature life-sorrow of the mother.

> Sleep sleep, happy sleep,
> While o'er thee thy mother weep.

113

> Sweet babe in thy face,
> Holy image I can trace.

Through the identity of maker and babe, in the sorrow of creativity, infant smiles become the fulfillment of life's pain. As always in Blake, as always in true myth, the vision projected is the material fulfillment of tendencies that burst through the laws of matter and logic when they are not impeded. They seem miraculous because we see them from the perspective of restrictive consciousness, where we take for granted a sterile destiny, but the miraculous is what happens when we let reality be itself, when we lift the anxieties of control. Then the truth seems strikingly simple and self-contained, for it is organic, existing only to unfold its own nature and confirm its existence in continuity.

Innocence does not exclude the harsher facts of life but embraces them. As Blake told Crabb Robinson, "There is suffering in Heaven; for where there is the capacity of enjoyment, there is the capacity of pain."[10] The point becomes a definition of freedom in "The Auguries of Innocence":

> Man was made for Joy & Woe
> And when this we rightly know
> Thro the World we safely go

In the songs, the little boy who is found by God in his father's form has also been abandoned by his father. The angels of "Night" are not supposed to prevent the slaughter of lambs.

114

When wolves and tygers howl for prey
They pitying stand and weep;
Seeking to drive their thirst away,
And keep them from the sheep.
But if they rush dreadful;
The angels most heedful,
Recieve each mild spirit,
New worlds to inherit.

The children of Innocence can be killed, and their death can be understood within the context of their innocence, for the wolves and tigers howling for prey are natural creatures too, driven by their own wild thirst. The angels would seem to be weeping in pity for the victims but we are told simply that "They pitying stand and weep." The less said, the more meaning, for the qualitative link is all the stronger. The angels must be aware of the predators' thirst as well as the lambs' danger and, beyond both, of the essentially unmoral nature of the situation. The cynic will complain of cause for small thanks, but it is not the function of true myth to change life, merely to chart the course of our reconciliation with it. Innocence integrates the "facts of life" by stylizing them with the touch of benediction.

It is a mistake to take the bloodshed of this song or the various manifestations of life's grief in other songs as manifestations of Experience, incursions from an outside world of "reality." Neither world is outside or in, and it is not the harsh facts that constitute Experience, but an attitude towards them. Myth is not concerned, as traditional science is, with grasping an objective reality detached from an observer, a god's-eye view in fact. The myth-maker represents reality only as his experience of

115

it. He is always a phenomenologist, projecting the psyche's qualitative perception of the world. He sees the world outside of him, the changing seasons, for instance, but he sees it as his phenomenon. In seeing, he projects the nature of vision itself. Myth projected by the psyche, that is to say, projects the nature of the psyche. In the cycle of seasons, the succession of generations, the passage through the stages of life, the psyche relates to its own rhythm.[11]

In "reconciling us to reality," therefore, myth transforms our resistance into love. Our alienated, objectifying mentality is dissolved. Our anxieties, aversions and terrors relax and when they do, they are no more. Thus all myth is innocent in technique (we say, usually, primitive or naive) and fulfills itself in innocence of vision. Or, to reverse the thought, innocence is the clarification of reality. Its proper language is myth, which clarifies reality, cleanses the doors of perception, by affirming our relationship with it. And it affirms reality not merely by recognizing and endorsing it but by making the relationship happen, again. The state it produces is its only subject; myth dissolves separation.

4. Experience, by Contrast

The obvious difference between "The Lamb" and "The Tyger" is the difference between a placid, mild creature and a fierce one, between passivity, therefore, and violence. But the essential difference between a Song of Innocence and a typical Song of Experience is not merely a difference in subject. It is the difference between the condition of consciousness (the "state of the human soul," as Blake indicates in his subtitle) that each dramatizes and therefore symbolizes. Both poems define creature and creator as they must be known in terms of each other. In "The Lamb" the question, "Who made thee?", is hardly asked at all. It is raised gently as a rhetorical framework to be fulfilled in a comforting answer, as an act of love. In "The Tyger" the imaginative energy is directed primarily at the attempt to visualize the unvisualizable attributes of an absolute that is just beyond grasp, frustrating and tantalizing: the immortal hand or eye, the deeps or skies, the wings of a being with hands, the brute musculature of pure force, the workshop that can forge a brain and, finally, the frame of mind that encounters such a product of its own will. The mind cannot even grasp its own questions, so

117

strong is the impression of what it confronts directly. Is the chain the flesh being hammered, is it a hoist to raise the bodily material onto the anvil or is it a restraint for the energy that is being unleashed? As with the identity of the shoulder (Is it creature's or creator's?) the distinction does not materialize.

The state of Experience that the poem defines is its particular quality of questioning. It would be wrong to say either that the questions can or cannot be answered, nor is their import agnostic. They mythologize, precisely and vividly, a pointedly nonvisual image that projects the tone of the questioning, a tone beyond awe and short of horror, at once pained and exhilarated, intensely enlivened by its own daring in pressing the questions as far as they will go. One is struck by the disjunction between hammers, chains and forge on the one hand and, on the other, living muscle and living energy. The combination is violent and painful. Yet this disjunction expresses appropriately the powers that threaten to overwhelm us because we are unconscious of them. Experience is the uneasy feeling of living in their shadow, at home in an alien land.

There are two questions asked, which project two ineffable relationships: What is the creator to the creature in the world of Experience, and What am I to this phenomenon of their relationship? In trying to grasp the first relationship, I establish the second. But the real trick is that on another level, I (W. B. as poet and I as reader) am just now making the beast and in confronting him, he is making me--that is, me as my experience of him. Somehow, the power of my life is the power of tyger-making.

The tyger is itself such a dynamic source of power that one cannot grasp a source beyond it; yet one must, for such force without a context implies irremediable chaos, absolute death. The salvation of the fallen Man, Albion, is possible in Jerusalem because with Adam and Satan are established the two limits to his fall. Fallen life is a maimed organism, but organic it still is and it will exist. One of the finest qualities of Blake's vision, recorded particularly in the great laments of The Four Zoas and the illustrations to The Book of Urizen, is his dual sense of both the vitality and the agony of fallen life, an agony all the more appalling because it is the effect of immense energy twisted pathetically against itself. This is the stars, who are also the fallen angels, throwing down their spears and watering heaven (like a garden, that it might flower?) with their tears.

Yet "The Tyger" does not give a clear sense that the creature of the forest is itself fallen; his situation seems to be, rather, something more ambiguous: that of an immense and thoughtless, amoral force of life which is capable of the devastation of a fall and also of lying down, like the lion, with the lamb (Blake's drawing of an ingenuous tiger seems, in most of the prints, playfully innocent). The song is emphatic on one point, surely: what is fearful is the creature's symmetry. It is a symmetry that can go in either direction, towards violence or play. It must be dynamic or it would not be fearful. One thinks of a symmetry between fire's warmth and light on one hand and its power to hurt, dessicate and consume. One thinks of symmetry between maker and made. Most directly, in the image itself, there is a balance of strange tension between the poise of symmetry and the uneasy fear it evokes. In its symmetry, the tyger is immensely, overwhelmingly coherent. But this is not the reassuring coherence of rational systematization. Before such coherence as this the mind ceases to function. It is not the coherence of beatitude, and surely not the coherence of morality; the only moral question remotely implied is whether a creator ought to do all he dare, the question of Macbeth and of Robert Oppenheimer. But the moral mind too (in both play and poem) watches helpless before the sheer energy that reduces it to irrelevance.

In terms of the dramatic process of the monologue, what the poem is about is the development of a vision that leads from the "could" of the first stanza to the "dare" of the last; it is the realization of a growing disjunction between the questioning mind and the reality it would confront. In the end, the original framework is transcended. The maker is not to be known by his capacity after all, but by his daring. The mind that has been thinking in terms of mechanics now flows over in apotheosis. As the entire image comes to burn brighter and brighter in the darkness of our minds, the wonder at means climaxes to become its own subject, wonder wondering, for the nature of life is essentially its sheer impracticality, its sheer self-sufficiency, its sheer disregard for niceties and scruples--its very sheerness. That tone between awe and horror emerges as the natural response to

120

this transcendence, or the natural vehicle for it. Since we can no longer ask about <u>coulds</u>, we can no longer properly ask any questions at all. The apparent question with which we conclude must satisfy itself, as awe and horror do, with their own utterance as an absolute statement.

5. The Innocence of "Innocence"

What makes "The Tyger" seem the essential Song of Experience is its effortful grappling with a reality that may or may not be within but that is beyond control. It is a response to the tragic burden: one must be confounded by life in order to be true to it. In the Songs of Innocence, all that needs to be known can be known. The world is a place where all of us creatures and forces belong together. Deity pervades all being with beneficence and ecstasy. It is a common mistake, however, to take this myth literally and assume that the many parental figures betoken a state of immature dependency. What is projected is the sense that life should be precisely what it is. The representation of a god outside man, which Blake elsewhere condemns as idolatry, is simply a stylized expression of a positive relation between one's self and one's universe. Blake here accepts a traditional image, as he does all the images of Christian pastoralism in the songs; he accepts them with a heightened innocence, granting them freely as much credit as they can carry. Thus the state of innocence is conveyed through an innocent rhetoric, which builds a myth accurate to its impulse on a basis of innocent logic, innocent

122

psychology, innocent sociology, innocent morality, innocent theology. The effect is a joyful generosity of spirit.

There is no separation possible between psychology and morality in "On Anothers Sorrow," and this unity is the whole point:

> Can I see anothers woe
> And not be in sorrow too.
> Can I see anothers grief,
> And not seek for kind relief.
> . . .
> Can a mother sit and hear,
> An infant groan and infant fear--
> No no never can it be.
> Never never can it be.

What comes to the mind of the psychological realist is, within the mentality of the poem, unthinkable. Appropriate feeling is made to feel natural and it must be true. It is beautiful and wholesome, utterly desirable and utterly dependable. Happily, what must be true, is true. The "Auguries of Innocence" is similarly a bold, even ritualistic, projection of innocent logic:

> He who shall hurt the little Wren
> Shall never be belovd by Men
> He who the Ox to wrath has movd
> Shall never be by Woman lovd

In "On Another's Sorrow" the natural innocence of a mother's instinct is the model of all living responses. The existence of a need, or of a sorrow, produces spontaneously a sympathetic

123

hearer. As a vacuum draws in air, pain draws love. The tone of the lyric, earnest and tender, precludes any alternative. There is no longer possible a question of how one should respond or an objection that one does not respond that way all too often. Joining the voice, one touches a level on which it all is simply true. In one's dearest self, it is true.

"The Little Black Boy," "Holy Thursday," and "The Chimney Sweeper" are full of opportunities for the realist to expose absurdities or, if he wishes to be sympathetic, to read the lines backwards to defensible ironies. The chimney sweeper content with his lot may disturb one's own sense of social justice, yet the tone of the poem is violated if one reads it in outrage. Its counterpart in Experience is ready to serve that need. The sweep's advice to the little newcomer, Tom Dacre, seems like the self-manipulation of despair:

> Hush Tom never mind it, for when your head's bare,
> You know that the soot cannot spoil your white hair.

Much good it should do the child that the hair he no longer has cannot be fouled! Yet this maneuver is not platitudinous, manipulative, absurd or childish. In its stylistic context, it is innocent logic. It delineates the order of how things should be, not socially but mythically. It is, for one thing, magic, the application of spiritual terms to physical reality. Transfigured by sacrifice, the shorn locks are more than real. What counts mythically is not the social reference out of the poem, but the state of mind inwardly. The Songs of Experience draw external

124

reality into them, but here the world is impervious to fact because it is emotionally perfect. The child's faith cannot be evaluated theologically or metaphysically either. It is all myth, projecting a pure joy, a clear sense of living affirmatively in a world where equity is not to be thought of. Equity is not only impossible, it is irrelevant. A fallen world is transformed only by a risen consciousness.

The movement of the poem concludes with an epitome of innocent ethics:

And so Tom awoke and we rose in the dark
And got with our bags & our brushes to work.
Tho' the morning was cold, Tom was happy & warm,
So if all do their duty, they need not fear harm.

The music of the verse works together with the mythic force of the little tale to assimilate an expedient doctrine into its solemn but beatific vision. Music itself is innocent, free of direct reference, and the meaning of these lines has the logic of song. The musical delight of form flowing along is another aspect of what the songs are all about. Myth absorbs into its qualitative form all manner of linear formulations. Theology, ethics, history and science all provide material which must be read in a new light when it reappears not as idea or fact or belief or advice, but as elements of an organism responsive to direct experience. The result is self-sustained delight, an overflowing of the self "for no good reason" but its own prolific existence. It is the strength of safety with which we could go through the world if we knew,

125

firmly and deeply, that we are made for joy and woe, inevitably fused. Experience is the attempt to separate them, to create with Urizen a world of joy only, of rational sense and practical convenience--which results, of course, in catastrophe only, in a morbid fear of pain and a present of perpetual anxiety. In Experience we are surprised each time "marks of woe" are encountered; and they are "appalling," very importantly so. The bard's human stature depends upon his ability to be appalled.

Commentaries on the "Holy Thursday" of Innocence usually assert that it must mean the opposite of what it says. Blake must be protesting here, as he does in the parallel Experience song, against the pious victimization of the charity children. Yet there is nothing present in the poem, taken by itself, to question the sincerity of its literal picture--a flower-river of ecstatic children guarded by benevolent seers. Taken together with its counterpart in Experience, the ingenuous mentality of this piece is even more striking. Tonally it is continuous with the rest of its own cycle, Innocence. Perhaps it represents a deliberate effort to see an unpleasant phenomenon with the eyes of innocence. At any rate, it mythologizes the situation by extending utter good faith where there has been none before. What is seen is taken at face value, on its own terms, but the result is not superficial. The facts are not here important for themselves, only the love of the beholder. He does not need to justify or condemn; he simply encounters a human tableau and is touched by it. As in "The Chimney Sweeper," the tag ending is an innocent gesture, summing up not ethics or expedient caution but revelation.

126

Then cherish pity, lest you drive an angel from your door

If it is directed at the not-so-wise real-life guardians of the really despised poor, it is directed as well at the reader on behalf of the corrupt guardians. Is it not at least an act of pity to call them "wise"? If there is a place for righteous wrath, there is another place for selfless trust in the humanity of all. The name of that place is Innocence.

Myth (and dreaming) makes the world look like what it feels like. It stylizes objective reality out of its temporal and spatial forms, out of its laws of causality and continuity and the rule of identity which separates subject and object, self and other, man and nature, feeling and fact. The life of the myth is grasped subjectively by a participation in its form in order to affirm the very real subjectivity of our experience. We affirm that life as we know it is our experience of life.

One of the principal techniques of Blake's mythmaking is cultivation of mergers and coalescence. In Experience and the Fall, the coalescences are horrific and nightmarish, evoking instability or evasiveness, a devouring of identity and a swelling violence:

> She lives upon his shrieks & cries
> And she grows young as he grows old
>
> Till he becomes a bleeding youth
> And she becomes a Virgin bright

> Then he rends up his Manacles
> And binds her down for his delight
> ("The Mental Traveller")

In Innocence coalescence is the emergence of wholeness from levels of reality that would seem distinct to the rational mind. There is a kind of love among apparently disparate facts.[12]

> For a Tear is an Intellectual Thing
> And a Sigh is the Sword of an Angel King
> ("The Grey Monk")

The child is the lamb is the maker. The black boy and the white become the same before God. My bosom becomes a cradle for sparrow and robin while a blossom that has no identity happily sees both the joy of the one bird and the sorrow of the other, taking in their existence with the perfection of utter simplicity. The old folk become one with the children as the play on the green surrounds them with both an echoing present and an echoing past until time yields calmly to the darkening green. Life fades into death. Lover fades into lover. Man fades into God. The reader becomes the singer as the singer becomes the song. Because the infant is joyful it _is_ joy, and because it is joy, its name is Joy. The individual _is_ the essence and the symbol _is_ the reality it represents. The flow of identity is complete freedom and that is itself the infant's joy.

All of the fictional paraphernalia--shepherds, lambs, cherubic children and wise guardians--are at the service of the tone and consciousness from which they emerge. They are

128

Infant Joy

I have no name
I am but two days old. —
What shall I call thee?
I happy am
Joy is my name, —
Sweet joy befall thee!

Pretty joy!
Sweet joy but two days old,
Sweet joy I call thee:
Thou dost smile.
I sing the while
Sweet joy befall thee.

"Infant Joy"   *British Museum*

129

functional, like all symbols, giving back the feelings that project them. The meaning of a myth can only be obscured, therefore, by probing along a one-to-one relation between the images and the data of the objective world. A new reality is created in the myth, reflecting a level of truth that has always existed. In an obvious sense, surfaces of this reality are spectacularly immaterial, but it is not a reality of stuff at all. Neither is it vague or wishful or hypothetical or esthetic. It is the image of a precise and immensely tangible state of being. If you call it ecstasy instead of innocence, or harmony or health, you substitute other names which point the way, but the quality itself must be known in experience (small e), as it arises through the perception of a myth, the mime of a ritual or the "conscious" voice of a lyric.

To read the Songs of Innocence ironically and sociologically is to be caught in the cyclical trap that the Songs of Experience prophesy against and that these songs circumvent. One feels inclined, perhaps, to explain away the racist assumptions implanted in "The Little Black Boy," but it does not help to do so entirely. It is true that the poem does, through the mother's lesson, affirm the equality of both selves (white and black), which must be freed of their cloud-like bodies at any rate; and it suggests that the black forest-child is stronger in God's ways than the civilized English boy. Yet the black boy does feel at a loss for his blackness and for his dependence on the white child, and he does need to affirm, in conventional terms, that his soul is white. Before God's knee, he gets to stroke the white boy's hair. The point of the poem, however, lies again in the innocence of the tone. The child _innocently_ accepts the violent impression of his inferiority and he accepts his own vulnerability in this spirit. He innocently turns to the mother who bore him and, under her instruction, to the father who would have him rejoice. Innocently he responds to her vision-lesson just as Tom Dacre responds to his dream. He responds, that is, spontaneously, from a self that unfolds to grow, manifesting its nature. And the singer of the song responds innocently to the whole phenomenon, touched warmly by the humanity he imagines.

6. Experience Beyond "Experience"

The innocent state is itself entirely positive; the intellect approaches it negatively by elimination. Ironical readings of the songs derive from a view that the Blakean Innocence is fragile and illusory, a world of pretty fantasies doomed to evaporate in the heat of reality. This view is cogent if one regards only the apparent surfaces of the lyrics but it fails to see the Innocent world as a stable mythical truth. It equates the innocence of these songs only with childhood, which must give way to mature disillusionment, or with a sheltered garden within a hostile world that sooner or later will be faced. But this is to see Innocence only in terms of Experience, to see reality as essentially chaotic. Problems that arise from this view are sometimes solved through a version of the Fortunate-Fall doctrine and a distinction between a higher and a lower Innocence located on either side of the Experience one must traverse to get from the one to the other. But it is important for Blake to deny such a distinction. When there is a higher and lower Innocence for Blake they are Beulah and Eden, both higher than the Ulro of the world and the Generation of the unregenerate flesh. Innocence, as it is

132

celebrated in the songs, is both our source and our destination. It is absolute, because it is total affirmation. Being eternal, how can it exist in any linear sequence? A note Blake made to his own manuscript of The Four Zoas, one that has been quoted a number of times, should preclude any assumption that innocence can be inadequate.

Unorganized Innocence, An Impossibility
Innocence dwells with Wisdom but never with Ignorance

The stylized world of the Songs is a triumph of organization.

There are two attitudes of "Experience" which contrast differently with Innocence. There is the pained wrath of the righteous prophet. This is itself a reflex of Innocence in response to Experience proper, the result of a commitment to the organic order of life. The bitterest satire is the most idealistic. And there is the grotesque pain of the jealous perverters of human nature. We are fully absorbed in the world of Experience in a poem like "A Poison Tree," which expresses one of Blake's most dramatic insights: the reason for our fallen state is our own protective interest in perpetuating it. The circularity of the mechanism explains why, from the fallen perspective, salvation must feel miraculous.

I was angry with my friend;
I told my wrath, my wrath did end.
I was angry with my foe:
I told it not, my wrath did grow.

133

This is not the prophet of "London" speaking, and the tone is not the irony of satire. It is more terrible than that. It is a frankly contented voice.

> In the morning glad I see;
> My foe outstretchd beneath the tree.

The reader may hear a tragic echo that is still a ways off, but if one detects guilt one is probably projecting it oneself. What is dramatized through the little monologue is importantly the consciousness of a self aware of its own temporary but very pleasant gratification. The profundity of the poem depends upon its objectivity in one sense: its simple confrontation of something problematic, a predicament not to be solved by moral or satiric judgment. In another sense it depends upon its subjectivity: I am trapped because I am gratified by my trap.

The psychology of Experience is familiar enough if we set aside our hopes of how we like to see ourselves. We can relate directly to it once we acknowledge our home in the nightmare. But between the Songs of Innocence and the Songs of Experience there is a necessary difference of method. It can be described as the difference in the mode of projection of each set of symbols. This factor tells us more about the meaning of symbols than any other. It is a concept related to style but more dynamic. It determines the symbolic ontology, the kind of reality the images maintain, and is itself determined by the psychic drives that generated them. It is a matter of how the self relates to its images. It is the difference between a wish out of frustration, a defense out of pride, a memory out of nostalgia and a fact out of curiosity. "A fool sees not the same tree that a wise man sees." What is literally the same image will differ in import in each instance. As we are, so we see; how we see therefore expresses what we are.

> God Appears & God is Light
> To those poor Souls who dwell in Night
> But does a Human Form Display
> To those who Dwell in Realms of day
> ("Auguries of Innocence")

The lambs and children of Innocence are not lambs and children unto themselves. It is notorious that a few illustrations to the songs show young (nude) adults where we would expect to find children. Nor are they not lambs and children. The images are both more and less than their referents. If Blakean lambs are symbolic of something human, yet real lambs still possess a distinctive "lamb"-like quality! If a child is born directly into "the dangerous world" of Experience "Like a fiend hid in a cloud" ("Infant Sorrow"), he is also, and at the same moment, the epitome of life's joy. And these lambs and babies are not metaphors for something other than themselves. Coleridge wrote, in The Statesman's Manual, "It is among the miseries of the present age that it recognizes no medium between literal and meta-phorical."[13] He is speaking of symbolism--we may say myth--and, of course, we are considerably more miserable, in his sense, today.

If in myth the psyche projects its own nature, myth is not about the contents of the psyche but its structure, the rhythm of

135

tension, frustration and potentiality that constitute the relationship between consciousness and unconsciousness. The central archetype is familiar enough: the hero dies by ordeal in traversing the underworld, in facing up to a monster, by resisting the totality of temptation or by undergoing the totality of pain in crucifixion--or by some other act symbolic of the impossible. Ordinary assumptions of possibility are challenged and what has been thought of as beyond human capacity turns out to be the essence of normality.

It is important that myth represents reality dynamically, through confrontation. Its truth is not told, it is revealed, it happens to one. The very multiplicity of myth, the endless variations on the themes, helps to make this possible, necessarily individuating the universal. Yet myth is analytical, for it projects, through the happening of a story, the essentially constant pattern of experiential reality, demonstrating relationships among its various aspects. In the Songs Blake achieves this effect through the cyclical confrontation of the two contrary states as well as within the drama of individual songs. One of the techniques of his prophecies is "simultaneous narrative," in which events occur without time transpiring. A constant "state" of life is analyzed by the symbolism of impulses, actions, and consequences; yet, in a dreamlike way, everything is always beginning and always ending. Different actions come both before and after each other. Personae exist only when they are thought of, although they are part of each other all the time. One's responses grow out of another's but induce the other's as well. Working in this way, Blake makes more apparent what is always implicit in archetypal myth: the birth, the adventure and the death of the hero all take place at the same moment and at every moment, just as the hero is all men and all men are one in Albion. The primary confrontation in the prophecies is with the self's own vision, as one manifests one's state of mind by dreaming it out--knowing the dream while being it, experiencing oneself as one's own projection.

The realization of our repression is simultaneously the realization of our potentiality. Blake's Thel is usually interpreted--looking backward from later works--as the voice of a limited Innocence, called Beulah, refusing the call of worldly Experience. (Blake's Beulah is ambiguously a state of ecstasy and of fallibility.) But if there is some validity to this standard reading, it does not really account for the state of mind the poem dramatizes. Thel may or may not be in any kind of Innocence, but what she rejects is not what Blake calls Experience. She sees the angels of "Night," as it were, and is "appalled" by their integrity. After a sincere but futile act of will (her name), she settles for repression and rejects wholeness.

We first see Thel, and identify with her, restless in the realization that there is something more to life than protective unconsciousness. The only one of the daughters of "Mne Seraphim" who is not content with an unreflective condition, she courageously asks the tragic question, Why must we bear the burden of mortality?

> Ah! Thel is like a watry bow, and like a parting cloud,
> Like a reflection in a glass. like shadows in the water.

The lily of the valley, the cloud and the clod of clay all exhort Thel with the natural Innocence that accepts death blithely, joyful in fact for the mortal bliss it makes possible. The maiden is drawn to the charm of their tender joy in transient being.

> I am a watry weed,
> And I am very small, and love to dwell in lowly vales;
> So weak, the gilded butterfly scarce perches on my head
> Yet I am visited from heaven and he that smiles on all.

She wanders among the dead solemnly and attentively until she comes to her own grave plot. Even there she sits down. But what she hears is more terrible than the thought of physical decay or the waste of temporality. She has been reconciled to being food for worms when she has seen the worm as an infant beloved by the nurturing clay. But the barrier that Thel cannot pass is the existential phenomenon, her consciousness of mortality. This includes her vulnerability to mortal psychology.

> Why cannot the Ear be closed to its own destruction?
> Or the glistning Eye to the poison of a smile!

The understatement is devastating. What keeps us mortal is far more subtle than physical decay. We are mortal because we know we are mortal.

The advice of lily, cloud and clod has been awesome because

of the leap required from our bodily self-consciousness to their spontaneous assumption of natural ecstasy. In the end, the leap is still too much. Thel retreats with a spontaneous shriek. The disjunction feels absolute and can be bridged only by means that feel miraculous. Her fear, however, is not mere cowardice. It measures the horror of what must be faced if organic beatitude is to flower. The voices of nature have told the girl her augury of innocence: we are born for joy and woe. She recoils with the reflex of Experience, for all the reasons that make "woe" sound, to the Experiential ear, like such a prettifying word.

7. The Relation of Contraries

As anyone knows who has done meaningful reading in the prophetic books, Blake's local symbols depend very much on their immediate context. They mean as they are seen, and they are seen <u>individually</u> as they are interpreted by a state of mind that they themselves develop collectively in a continuing transaction. The ultimate effect of Blake's mythmaking is to evoke, in fact, an eminently fluid sense of existence--"organiz'd" by its nature rather than by the nature of conceptualizing language, concrete images and logical principles of identity. It is especially unsafe, therefore, to read the state of mind developed in one work in terms of states developed elsewhere. Often it can be done fruitfully, sometimes it can not. One must go back through the projector's beam of light to know. Blake's visions are difficult to grasp for the very reason that he did not normally allow his vivid sense of reality to become oversimplified by his system. To avoid being enslaved by others, he needed not only a new system, as he claimed, but a new conception of what system is.

Blake's various structures representing levels of reality--

Heaven:Hell, Prolific:Devourer, Ulro:Generation:Beulah:Eden--are all schema that overlap in significance but each resolves a special need. Innocence may be reformulated in later works, with reference to other dimensions of its nature, in order to resolve particular problems posed by other contexts, but The Songs of Innocence and of Experience is a complete system, representing the two contrary states. They neither refer to nor imply any further condition. The nature of Blake's "contrary" relationship does not itself seem stable. In The Marriage of Heaven and Hell there never develops a very cooperative kind of marriage. The work does produce two patterns, however: one by which the devil converts (and therefore subsumes) the angel and another by which the prolific requires that the devourer remain distinct for his own sustenance ("Opposition is true Friendship"). These two versions of "marriage," it seems, are themselves contrary truths. Neither is a Hegelian dialectic leading to a further stage; each is definitive and so is the difference between them.

In a world driven by the unconsciousness we share inevitably with all others, we have a need to respect the problematic order of disorder in Experience. In this sense Experience is as absolute as the darkness that surrounds our lives to which we return each night. Yet we have a responsibility to ourselves, being persons living in the present, to say that life is absolute and death a chimera. As the voice of clear consciousness, Innocence integrates Experience and passes it by. Experience is real and tangible to us, as troubled dreams are real. Most of us have little cause to believe we will ever feel at home elsewhere. Yet we can

Title page to   *British Museum*
Experience

recognize the negativity of those fears and gratifications that hold us bound in the desperate cycle of "The Mental Traveller" or in "The Golden Net." We can sense that Experience is frustration, a holding back, "mind-forg'd manacles," implying something else that is positive, a natural condition, which we negate.

Innocence, again, does not change reality in itself. At the end of the song, the little black boy still longs for the love of the English boy. It merely asserts a clearer relation to reality, through a clearer relation with oneself. The "meaning" that life has is the assertion of such relationship with one's own experience. To ask the question, to seek for meaning, is to be on the hither side of the transition, to exist like Hamlet interrogatively, to be, as we say, "alienated." The question is answered by its transcendence. Thus the meaning of life itself is not a philosophical problem but the function of a process or activity-- properly a dramatic or a mythic problem.

In the Songs, Innocence is expressed by a perfect quality of poise. To the restless nerves of Experience, this perfection seems static and lifeless. But it is flat only in the sense that deity and heaven, the pastoral and the romance, require a flat stylization by their very nature. The infinite is perfect with its own fullness. The tensions of the world resolve here, appropriately--not in rest, however, but in play, a fluency of energy in absolute delight. The world that seems superficially an escapist fantasy, in its spirit defines our fullest nature. It relates to Experience as answer relates to question, as solution to problem, as satisfaction to need.

Innocence is the timeless moment of catharsis and the eternity after the tragedy is over, as well as the source of life in childlike potentiality. It is the rejection of time when one "kisses the joy as it flies."

8. The Meaning of Perspective

The Romantic poet projects the world he knows he needs in order to fulfill himself. In a different way, Blake, as a visionary, sees and records what is in front of his eyes, stripped bare of the veil of mortality--"as it is, infinite." The difference in attitude between Blake and the typical English Romantics is a difference not in vision so much as in the relation to vision, which is all the difference between an idealist and a realist in the common usage of the words. We see again and again in Shelley, Wordsworth, Coleridge and Keats the willful effort to realize a transcendent or integrative state of mind: hence Romantic disillusionment and dejection, for frustration and dream are reflexes of one another. Blake is beyond this, piping his merry tunes and his painful ones to those who will hear, gratuitous messages from the land of the living. Clearly this man knew in his life a man's share of frustration and disappointment--arguably of bitterness--and for reasons easy to appreciate. He was not a saint, but he was a prophet. He knew where his home was and he was glad to live there when he could, alone if he was alone.

145

The difference between Blake's prophecies and Prometheus Unbound is the difference between truly analytical myth and Utopian fiction. Blake portrays what is in terms of what makes it be what it is. In Shelley we observe the hard-fought struggle to create a new order. It is a truly heroic act of raising oneself by one's own bootstraps, but at the end one feels a little unreal about hovering six inches off the ground. One remembers Ozymandias and despairs, trapped in time, substance and pride.

Shelley's skylark is projected in order to be unattainable: I would surpass myself with only

> half the gladness
> That thy brain must know . . .

Compelled as we are by "sweetest songs . . . that tell of saddest thought," our fulfillment is escape and wish:

> Yet if we could scorn
>   Hate, and pride, and fear;
> If we were things born
>   Not to shed a tear,
> I know not how thy joy we ever should come near.

Such joy cannot be human, for it does not, as Blake's does, admit sorrow. The last lines of Prometheus Unbound indicate that the whole work is a spell against reality, to be used if we should happen to lapse from a transcendence that does exist only in the poem:

And if, with infirm hands, Eternity,
Mother of many acts and hours, should free
The serpent that would clasp her with his length;
These are the spells by which to reassume
An empire o'er the disentangled doom.

The essence of the whole work is crystallized in the specific concluding spells, a pledge of determined endurance and loving optimism:

To love, and bear; to hope, till Hope creates
From its own wreck the thing it contemplates . . .

out of which derives all that is glorious:

This is alone Life, Joy, Empire, and Victory.

The propaganda is valuable, but it should be distinguished from celebration.

The heaven that Adonais attains is likewise the product of the poet's poetic effort, self-sustained. It is a conceit willed into metaphysics by vatic authority: as a poet I see hidden truth, I have said it is true, therefore it becomes true. My words conjure it, I have spoken, there it is. The image exists within a consciousness of its own artificiality. We extrapolate: it must be so, therefore it is so--and the poem is meaningful to us because we do agree that it must be so. Beyond the "dome of many-colored glass" there must be "white radiance" or we would not see the glass so clearly. Still the result is fiction; it has the truth of a proposition as it were. How far do we trust a metaphor?

Innocence and Experience are significantly different from Romantic ecstasy and dejection. The state of consciousness each expresses assumes a different base of normality. The Romantic grasps intensely the usual assumptions of the way we live: normality is frustration, fulfillment a dream. Though he "believes in" something better, he remains committed to his fallen world. He knows intense well-being as a transient state but regards it as the absolute from a perspective. The belief may not be derived by intellectual processes, yet looking towards the absolute from afar, he often relates to it as though it were known by inference. To the truly visionary, however, the self exists naturally in fulfillment. The healthy organic process is simple and immediate; normality is ecstasy. All else is shadow, life manqué. The Romantic may say the same thing, but he says it in order to discover that it is true. He knows that it must be so but he does not know that it is so. The visionary or mystic overflows with his knowledge. It is a difference, again, in the mode of projection, and it is one that makes all the difference between life and death, between Innocence, that is, and Experience.

APPENDIX

SOME CULTURAL ASSUMPTIONS

In order to perceive some of the assumptions that Blake makes, and that myth and tragedy also derive from, it may help to reflect on other assumptions that we make ordinarily as subjects of a culture. Some characterize Western culture in particular, others perhaps any culture at all.

I. General

1. We are born into reality, observe it, learn to control it. The mind grasps forms and categories that exist as characteristics of things outside the mind (the mind being inside reality, which is outside).

2. Whatever is most difficult to change or control is most real. Matter being inert and tangible, not (to ordinary appearances) changing spontaneously, is the basis for reality. Life is an activity of matter.

3. The mind is not in itself real; nevertheless, the most dignified pursuit of man is the cultivation of his mind. The body is not in itself good, but it is real; the mind is not in itself real, but it is good.

4. Rationality is the mind's link with reality, which requires a link since it is outside. We speak justly of the rational mind, which can be distinguished, fortunately, with some effort of concentration, from the irrational mind. The bases of rationality are: a) objective description, which has a validity that immediate experience has not; b) the avoidance or elimination of contradictions; c) the tracing of tangible cause-effect relations; d) the charting of paths to goals; e) applying dualistic distinctions to different dimensions of life.

5. Life is good, we are grateful to be alive; yet we must not expect too much from life. Maturity is the accumulation of responsibilities as well as the realization of ultimate limitations. Virtue is the effort by which we counteract the natural force of life to pull us down into the painful, morbid, disruptive aspects of life. Wisdom is cautionary--the knowledge of human limits and the resignation to them, the avoidance of those negative qualities we gravitate towards. We have a moral responsibility to choose between the alternatives that the rational mind delineates (see 4,e).

6. Outside the physical realm, where experimentally verifiable data is <u>factual</u> (and the historical realm, where we are entitled to pretend the same), all "knowledge" and interpretation of reality is relative and tentative, basically an aspect of personality, whether the result of social conditioning or idiosyncratic invention.

7. Meaning is given to life by philosophies that order life's own

natural chaos or give character to its indeterminacy. People are entitled to confidently "believe" their interpretations, whether in "schools of thought" or, to a lesser extent, in isolation (this being an enlightened culture), but not to take their confidence too seriously. "Beliefs" are in themselves arbitrary, but the consciousness of holding them endows them with the sanctity of absolutes.

8. Everything exists through the media of time and space, which give things their unique identities and delimitations. Time is a succession of moments. Eternity is a) an endless succession of moments or b) the condition before and after time, which may be conceived of as an interruption of eternity. Space is a continuum of specific places, each of which remains forever fixed and distinct, set off by artificial boundaries.

9. Wisdom is measured by efficiency (and economy of effort). The most successful course is the safest. Wisdom therefore lies in self-control, moderation--the balancing of tendencies rather than the pursuit of any at the expense of others or at the risk of any loss. This principle applies to both practical and intellectual endeavors.

10. Dignity is given to life by purposeful efforts. A goal can be a reason for being, although being is a given condition and a goal is an achievement posited in the future by the will.

11. One's fundamental being is his personality, the combination of

traits acquired and cultivated in response to (or reaction against) the standards held up by family and society. One must have an admirable personality, yet one should be known by his individuality, his apparently unique characteristics, especially if he is oneself. One should be unique, however, in an acceptable way.

12. The best people are the most agreeable: the considerate, the pleasant; those who are constructive without being critical, who hold the social group together by substantiating its assumptions. One is respected if one is respectable. To be respected for having something, one must deserve it; one deserves through work, patience, deprivation or simply good (unobtrusive) behavior. Character is the degree of success with which one achieves the standards of the group.

13. Civilization affords man the wherewithal to bolster his natural self--with the dignity of achievements, powers, properties, virtues and adornments. Art is a deliberate form of exaggeration and thereby, at its best, an exciting ornament to life, flattering to the possessor or perceiver, a reminder of one's own high ideals and standards of taste. It may be of great value, because of the refinement it superadds to life.

II. The Literary Symbol

1. The symbol is a substitute for something else or it is a pleasing object in itself. It is a means towards an end or an end in itself

isolated from the rest of experience. It is a tool to communicate an idea more important than itself. It is a pretence at direct communication, disguising a hidden meaning.

2. The poem (etc.) is an artifact to be observed and judged. It has identity, unity and significance (see Joyce on Aquinas), cohering as a complete thing in itself though colored by the life that produced it. Because it comments on life metaphorically, the critic can approach it either as image or commentary, esthetically or philosophically, whichever suits his convenience or produces the happiest results. The decorum of the work preserves its integrity as a thing, discreet and tangible, to which one may address oneself as critic.

3. Everything that enters into the literary work becomes fiction. It is then arbitrary in relation to reality, functioning as metaphor in order to be instructive. Its fictive nature insulates the symbol from reality and vice versa. It has charm and self-importance but remains a pretence or a game.

NOTES

The Celebration of Disaster

1. From The Bacchae, translated by William Arrowsmith, and Oedipus the King, translated by David Grene, both in The Complete Greek Tragedies, edited by David Grene and Richmond Lattimore (Chicago, 1955); and Hippolytus, translated by Philip Vellacott, in Alcestis and Other Plays (Harmondsworth and Baltimore, 1953).

2. "The poet's task is, of course, not to copy life but to organize and articulate a symbol for the 'sense of life' . . . Susanne Langer, Feeling and Form (N.Y., 1953), p. 363.

3. The puzzle that tragedy appears only in Western culture even though it seems universal is resolved simply by George Steiner:
    > All men are aware of tragedy in life. But tragedy as a form of drama is not universal. Oriental art knows violence, grief, and the stroke of natural or contrived disaster; the Japanese theatre is full of ferocity and ceremonial death. But that representation of personal suffering and heroism which we call tragic drama is distinctive of the western tradition. The Death of Tragedy (N.Y., 1961), p. 3, my italics.

4. Heinrich Zimmer, The King and the Corpse (Princeton, 1956, 2nd ed.), p. 307.

5. Northrop Frye, "The Argument of Comedy," originally in English Institute Essays, 1948, reprinted in Shakespeare: Modern Essays in Criticism, ed. by Leonard Dean (Oxford, 1967, rev. ed.), p. 84.

6. Joseph Campbell, The Hero with a Thousand Faces (N.Y., 1949), p. 28. In The Birth of Tragedy Nietzsche writes that "the primal ground of tragedy . . . represents . . . the

shattering of the individual and his fusion with primal being." Kaufmann translation (N.Y., 1967), p. 65.

7. Karl Jaspers, Tragedy is not Enough (Archon Books reprint, 1969), p. 76.

8. Robert Heilman, "Tragedy and Melodrama: Speculations on Generic Form," The Texas Quarterly, Summer 1960, pp. 36-50; see also Arthur Miller, "The Shadow of the Gods," Harpers, August 1958, pp. 35-43. Heilman's essay was expanded into a book, Tragedy and Melodrama: Versions of Experience (Seattle, 1968).

9. Jaspers writes in exposition of this theme:
> I am responsible for all the evil that is perpetrated in the world, unless I have done what I could to prevent it, even to the extent of sacrificing my life. I am guilty because I am alive and can continue to live while this is happening. Thus criminal complicity takes hold of everyone for everything that happens.

He distinguishes, however, two kinds of tragic guilt:
> First: Existence is guilt. Guilt in the larger sense is identical with existence as such. The idea, already found in Anaximander, recurs in Calderon, although in a different sense--that man's greatest guilt is to have been born. Tragedy is not Enough, p. 53.
>
> . . .
>
> Second: Action is guilt . . . Man cannot escape his guilt through right and truthful conduct: guilt itself seems incurred guiltlessly. Man takes this guilt upon himself . . . p. 55.

Schopenhauer developed the theme earlier. See the handy brief history of tragic theory in the first part of Raymond Williams' Modern Tragedy (London, 1966).

10. Zimmer, p. 49.

11. Theorists seem to have taken us well beyond the tragic-flaw logic by now, although it will continue to provide convenient essay topics and exam questions. Although it means little, it

is eminently communicable. Existential philosophers (after the lead of Hegel, Schopenhauer and Nietzsche) have helped focus on the tragic communication, rather than on the fictional structure, following the radical assumption that tragedy is about the nature of human existence. See for example: Susanne K. Langer, Feeling and Form (New York, 1953); Roy Morrell, "The Psychology of Tragic Pleasure," Essays in Criticism (January, 1956); Richard B. Sewall, The Vision of Tragedy (New Haven and London, 1959); A.P. Rossiter, Angel with Horns (London, 1961); Oscar Mandel, A Definition of Tragedy (New York, 1961); George Steiner, The Death of Tragedy (New York, 1961); Thomas McFarland, Tragic Meanings in Shakespeare (New York, 1966); Walter Kaufmann, Tragedy and Philosophy (New York, 1968); Clifford Leech, Tragedy (London, 1969); Laurence Michel, The Thing Contained: Theory of the Tragic (Bloominton, London, 1970); Joyce Carol Oates, The Edge of Impossibility: Tragic Forms in Literature (N.Y., 1972). Langer, Morrell, Sewall, Oates, and several other writers I have cited-- Heilman, Frye, and Jaspers--can be found in Robert W. Corrigan's anthology Tragedy: Vision and Form, 2nd ed. (N.Y., 1981).

12.   An English translation of the play is available in Oedipus: Myth and Drama, edited by Martin Kallich, Andrew MacLeish and Gertrude Schoenbohm (N.Y., 1968).

13.   Perilous Balance: The Tragic Genius of Swift, Johnson and Sterne (Princeton, 1939), p. 6.

14.   In Electra and Other Plays, translated by E.F. Watling (Harmondsworth and Baltimore, 1943).

15.   Campbell, p. 16.

16.   The Tempest (London, 1954), p. lxii.

17.   Jaspers, p. 88.

18.   As a matter of fact, Aristotle is concerned throughout with the means that produce "the essential tragic effect," "the

true tragic pleasure" (Butcher trans.).

19. Northrop Frye, Anatomy of Criticism (Princeton, 1957), p. 208.

20. See John Holloway, "Shakespearean Tragedy and the Idea of Human Sacrifice," The Story of the Night (London, 1961), p. 149.

21. Reported by R.P. Blackmur? The anecdote makes a vital point about symbolism--both esthetic and, I should think, theological.

22. See Roy Morrell, "The Psychology of Tragic Pleasure."

23. The Politics of Experience and The Bird of Paradise (N.Y., 1967), p. 11; see also pp. 35ff.

24. The Statesman's Manual, excerpted in The Portable Coleridge, ed. by I.A. Richards (N.Y., 1950), p. 388.

25. "In symbol there is concealment and yet revelation: here therefore, by Silence and by Speech acting together, comes a double significance." Carlyle represents the tension in metaphysical terms: "Speech is of Time, Silence is of Eternity." Sartor Resartus, Book III, Ch. III, "Symbols." Ernst Cassirer speaks of the "dialectic of bondage and liberation, which the human spirit experiences with its own self-made image worlds . . ." The Philosophy of Symbolic Forms, Volume 2: Mythical Thought (New Haven, 1955).

26. Hermann Hesse, Steppenwolf, translated by Basil Creighton (N.Y., 1957), p. 59.

27. "To let the silence in is symbolism." Norman O. Brown, Love's Body (N.Y., 1968), p. 190. Brown quotes Carlyle.

28. Philosophy in a New Key (Cambridge, Mass., 1942), pp. 3f.

29. "For all Shakespeare's tragic heroes, words lose their meaning." M.M. Mahood, Shakespeare's Wordplay (London, 1957, reprinted 1968), p. 181.

Blake's Myth of Innocence

1. *The Philosophy of Literary Form* (N.Y., 1957, rev. ed.), p. 75.

2. Blake quotations are from David V. Erdman's edition, *The Poetry and Prose of William Blake* (N.Y., 1965, 1970).

3. George Starbuck, "On First Looking in on Blodgett's *Keats's* 'Chapman's *Homer*' (Sum. ½C. M9-11)," *Bone Thoughts* (New Haven, 1960).

4. In *A Vision of the Last Judgment* Blake cautions us to "Note here that Fable or Allgory is Seldom without some Vision Pilgrims Progress is full of it the Greek Poets the same but Allegory & Vision ought to be known as Two Distinct Things & so calld for the Sake of Eternal Life," Erdman, p. 544.

5. Basil Busacca, "A Country Doctor," in *Franz Kafka Today*, ed. by Angel Flores and Homer Swander (Madison, 1958), pp. 45-54. Kenneth Burke writes in *Counter-Statement*: "The symbol is a formula." (Chicago, 1957, rev. ed., p. 153). In *The Philosophy of Literary Form*, referring to I.A. Richards, he makes the suggestive statement that "the symbolic act is the dancing of an attitude" (p. 9, his italics).

6. Erdman, p. 560.

7. Erdman, p. 544.

8. Erdman, p. 544. The editor's indication of deletions and additions has not been followed in this quotation and the next.

9. Erdman, p. 553.

10. Selections from Crabb Robinson's *Reminiscences*, in *The Portable Blake*, ed. by Alfred Kazin (N.Y., 1946), p. 683.

11. "Thus we see that for mythical consciousness and feeling a kind of biological time, a rhythmic ebb and flow of life, precedes the intuition of a properly cosmic time. . . . At

first the mythical consciousness apprehends the change of day into night, the flowering and fading of plants, and the cyclical order of the seasons only by projecting these phenomena into human existence, where it perceives them as in a mirror. This reciprocal relation gives rise to a mythical feeling of life and the objective intuition of nature." Ernst Cassirer, The Philosophy of Symbolic Forms, Volume 2: Mythical Thought (New Haven, 1955), p. 109. See Cassirer's discussion of Schelling in the "Introduction: The Problem of a Philosophy of Mythology." Schelling writes: "It is not with things that man has to do in the mythological process, it is powers arising within consciousness itself that move him." (Quoted on p. 8, with italics.) And: "Mythology is recognized in its truth and hence truly recognized in its process; and the process which is repeated in it, though in a particular way, is the universal, absolute process." (Quoted on p. 12.).

12. A similar effect can be seen in medieval lyrics such as "Now goth sonne under wod" and "I sing of a maiden / That is makeless."

13. The Portable Coleridge, ed. by I.A. Richards (N.Y., 1950), p. 388. The point about Blake's children (and lambs) will come as no surprise to readers familiar with Jung's essay "The Psychology of the Child Archetype" (reprinted in Violet S. de Laszlo, ed., Psyche and Symbol, Garden City, 1958).

Racine, Jean, 34f.
Richard II, 48, 50, 72.
Romantic poetry, 145-48.
Romeo and Juliet, 59.

satire and tragedy, 43-46.
Schelling, Friedrich W.J.,
   quoted, 159.
Seneca, 87.
Shakespeare, William. See
   individual plays.
Shelley, Percy Bysshe, 39,
   77, 145-48.
Sidney, Sir Philip, 53.
Sophocles. See individual
   plays.
Steiner, George, 154.
Steppenwolf, quoted, 81.
Strindberg, August, 24,
   88f.
supernatural in tragedy,
   46.
symbol defined, 103.

Tamburlaine, 58.
Tempest, The, 39.
Thel, The Book of, 137-39.
"tragic flaw" fallacy, 29,
   38, 43, 73.
"tragic subjunctive," 73-75.
Troilus and Cressida, 44f.,
   61.
"Tyger, The," 107, 117-122.

Urizen, The Book of, 119.

Vision of the Last Judg-
   ment, A, 106, 107, 158.

Waiting for Godot, 21.
Watkins, W.B.C., 44.

Way of the World, The, 44.
Webster, John, 59, 72.
Wheelwright, Philip, x.
Wild Duck, The, 45, 86, 88f.
Wings of the Dove, The, 63.
Women of Trachis, The, 49.

Zimmer, Heinrich, 16, 33.

About the Author

Harvey Birenbaum was an undergraduate at Antioch
College, receiving his B.A. in 1958, and a graduate
student at Yale, where he held a Woodrow Wilson Fellow-
ship and completed his doctoral work in 1963. In 1965
he began to teach at San Jose State University, where
he is now Professor of English. For the 1972-73 year,
he was Visiting Lecturer at the University of East
Anglia in England. He is also on the faculty of the
Psychological Studies Institute in Palo Alto. His
interest in the relation between consciousness and literature underlay his doctoral dissertation, a revision
of which is available from University Microfilms under
the title Stoic in Love: Convention and Self in the
Poetry of Wyatt. While writing Tragedy and Innocence
he began to apply its conception of literary experience
to the plays of Shakespeare in a study called The Art of
our Necessities. At this date, two chapters, which
elaborate upon the present views on tragedy, have ap-
peared in print: one on Hamlet (in Pacific Coast Phil-
ology, June 1981) and one on Macbeth (Mosaic, Summer
1982). The Yale Review will print a third, on King
Lear, in 1983. He has also been completing another
book, Myth and Mind, which develops the perspective on
myth suggested here. He intends to explore further the
role of symbolism in culture with a book to be called
Unfolding the Word.